STRANGE CREATURES

DAVID PETERS

MORROW JUNIOR BOOKS

NEW YORK

I'd like to thank David Reuther, Editor-in-Chief at Morrow Junior Books, for offering me the opportunity to create this book and for working with me to see it finished.

This book is dedicated to Tycho and Alex.

Acrylic was used for the full-color artwork. The text type is 11 point Garamond Light.

Printed in Hong Kong by South China Printing Company (1988) Ltd.

1 2 3 4 5 6 7 8 9 10

Library of Congress Cataloging-in-Publication Data
Peters, David, 1954–
    Strange creatures / David Peters.
        p.   cm.
    Summary: Describes a variety of outrageous and unique animals, many of which lived in prehistoric times.
    ISBN 0-688-10154-2 (trade).—ISBN 0-688-10155-0 (library)
    1. Animals—Juvenile literature. 2. Extinct animals—Juvenile literature.
[1. Animals. 2. Prehistoric animals.] I. Title.
QL49.P395 1992
591—dc20 91-36205 CIP AC

Contents

Introduction

Unique. Bizarre. Outrageous. Incredible. These are the words that will enter your mind as you look at the strange creatures in this book. Flip through the pages, and you are guaranteed to come across at least a few animals you have never heard of before. No, they're not the product of some artist's vivid imagination. All the animals in this book were once—or still are—real live animals.

Imagine a creature having a ring finger longer than its entire body. Of course this giant digit had to be folded backward like a ski pole whenever it was not being used. Another outrageous animal had a neck that was longer than the rest of its body. A third glided from branch to branch by stretching its legs; still another glided through the air by stretching its enormous rib cage.

The deep seas contain a fish that has two bodies. Another sea creature has eyeballs on the end of wavy stalks. A third waves a tiny lure that looks like the prey it is trying to entice.

There are fish that look like plants, two-legged crocodiles, elephants no bigger than puppies, and much, much more in this book of strange creatures.

On each page of this book the creatures are illustrated to the same scale; but the scale may vary from one double-page spread to the next. To give a visual impression of the actual sizes of the animals—whether tiny or gigantic—a five-foot-tall human is included in most of the illustrations. When the animals are illustrated to their actual sizes, humans are not included.

Aquatic animals are illustrated in the first part of the book. Terrestrial animals follow: first invertebrates, then vertebrates of increasing complexity, and finally primates. Extinct animals and living ones, including humans, may be shown on the same page, but this is not meant to suggest that they lived at the same time. Extinct creatures will always be identified as such.

Discovering these "critters" among the shelves of a dozen libraries and museums has been an exciting experience. Nevertheless, I'm sure my experience can't compare with the thrill of making the actual discovery of a new creature in the deep seas or the jungle or the rocks of some forsaken outcrop. Some people have made a career out of discovering new creatures.

Every newly discovered creature seems strange at first. As we get to know it better, the animal slowly becomes more familiar. Some of the animals in this book may not seem as bizarre as others you already know. But because many of them are either new to science or have never appeared in other popular books, they are included here—in some cases for the first time anywhere.

—D.P.

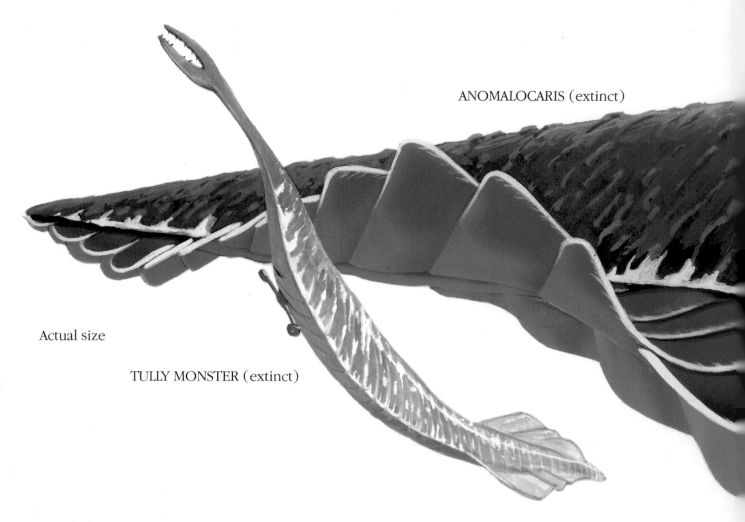

ANOMALOCARIS (extinct)

Actual size

TULLY MONSTER (extinct)

Incredible Invertebrates

Tullimonstrum (tul-i-MONS-trum), or the Tully monster, was a flattened, wormlike swimmer that lived 300 million years ago in the area that is now Illinois and grew up to a length of thirteen inches. In the front of its body was a claw or a mouth (scientists are not sure which) armed with tiny teeth. Most unusual was a stiff bar that crossed its body. On either end of this tiny bar there seems to have been an eye. No other known animal has eyes like these. In fact, the animals on these two pages have body parts and plans unlike those of any other known animals.

The following six animals all lived 500 million years ago in a sea that once covered western Canada.

Four separate parts of *Anomalocaris* (ah-nome-uh-loe-KARE-iss) were first identified as complete animals in themselves, until scientists realized that they all belonged together on one body. *Anomalocaris*, or "odd shrimp," was named for its feeding arms, which resembled shrimp. At almost two feet in length, this predator was a giant of its day. *Anomalocaris* had a mouth consisting of a circle of contracting plates. The inner border of each of these plates was toothed to break up hard-shelled prey. *Anomalocaris* swam the way a squid does, moving forward or backward with equal ease by waving its overlapping flaps in sequence.

Perhaps the weirdest animal of all time was the inch-long *Hallucigenia* (hal-oo-si-JEE-nee-uh), named for its "bizarre and dream-like appearance." It is impossible to determine which end is which, so the poorly preserved bulb at one end has been called the "head," and the "smokestack" at the other end has been called the "tail." Seven long tentacles and six smaller ones grew along the "back." Attached to its "underside" were seven pairs of sharply pointed spines, which seem to have served as walking legs. This freak of nature could

HALLUCIGENIA (extinct)

OPABINIA (extinct)

AMISKWIA (extinct)

6

not have moved rapidly, so it probably stayed put, feeding on plankton.

Opabinia (oh-puh-BIN-ee-uh) was a three-inch-long predator that grabbed its prey with a spiny clasper at the end of an elephantlike trunk. *Opabinia* used its trunk to pass food back to its mouth, which opened beneath its body. This strange swimmer had five eyes. Each segment of its body served as a base for a pair of swimming flaps and gills. These flaps formed oars that must have paddled the water like a Roman galleon or a Viking ship. The last three flaps formed a V-shaped rudder.

Amiskwia (ah-miss-KWEE-uh) was neither fish nor arrowworm; it had fins and tentacles unlike those of any other creature.

Odontogriphus (oh-don-tuh-GRIF-us), or "toothed riddle," was as flat as a pancake. Beneath the corners of its head were a pair of shallow sensory depressions that were probably smelling organs. Between the depressions was a tiny mouth surrounded by an open ring of tiny "teeth." It's possible that *Odontogriphus* punctured the skin of other animals and drank their body fluids.

Wiwaxia (wi-WAKS-ee-uh) was like a spiny snail, and like a snail it probably scraped algae off rocks with its special comblike teeth. This sea creature was armored with small overlapping plates and large, protruding spines. When it was time to grow, *Wiwaxia* would slip out of its old armor and grow a new set of plates and spines.

WIWAXIA (extinct)

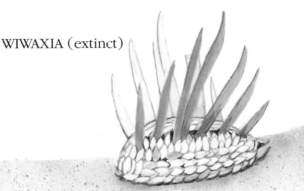

ODONTOGRIPHUS (extinct)

7

Sensational Sea Scorpions

Sea scorpions were long, streamlined, marine arthropods (jointed-legged invertebrates). They appeared during the Cambrian period, 540 million years ago, and became extinct during the Permian period, 300 million years later. Sea scorpions are most closely related to the living horseshoe crabs, scorpions, and spiders. These arthropods all have a body divided into two parts—a head/thorax and an abdomen. In each case, the head/thorax has six pairs of appendages. The five rear pairs are usually walking legs. The first pair, called chelicerae (kel-EES-eh-ray), are usually pincers that serve as mouth parts. Sea scorpions have only one pair of pincers. Land scorpions have two.

The innermost portions of the sea scorpion's legs surrounded the mouth. These "shoulder" segments were toothed to chew and tear food to bits by grinding against one another.

Plates of armor covered the top and bottom of sea scorpions. Feathery gills sprouted from the joints between each set of plates on the chest. By fanning them in unison, sea scorpions may have swum through the water upside down, the way horseshoe crabs do today. Most sea scorpions also had swimming paddles.

Typically, sea scorpions had two sets of eyes, a small pair on top and a larger pair in front.

Sea scorpions must have been very well adapted. Although not that many species are known, some existed for 100 million years or more.

Mixopterus (miks-OP-ter-us) fossils have been found in Ordovician, Silurian, and early Devonian rocks of eastern North America and Norway. During those periods these areas had no ocean separating them. *Mixopterus* had a body like a scorpion's. Its tail narrowed to a spike similar to a scorpion's poison gland. The two foremost sets of legs had long spikes for snaring and trapping smaller prey, such as fish. Perhaps these spikes pierced soft-bodied animals, which could then be eaten at leisure, like cubes of cheese on toothpicks. The next two pairs of limbs were normal in appearance and the rearmost set was flattened into swimming paddles.

Stylonurus (stye-loe-NOOR-us), the daddy long-legs of its day, was a contemporary of *Mixopterus.* The four rearmost legs of this five-foot-long giant were exceptionally large, probably for walking across the seafloor like a lobster. Another notable feature of *Stylonurus* was its long, sharp tail, or telson, similar to that of the living horseshoe crab. The telson

is used as a lever during digging and to help set the animal upright.

Pterygotus (tare-ee-GO-tus) lived during the same time and in the same places as *Mixopterus* and *Stylonurus*, and also in Australia. A few of these sea scorpions grew to seven feet in length, although most were about one foot long.

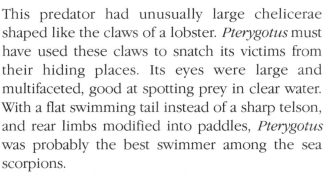

This predator had unusually large chelicerae shaped like the claws of a lobster. *Pterygotus* must have used these claws to snatch its victims from their hiding places. Its eyes were large and multifaceted, good at spotting prey in clear water. With a flat swimming tail instead of a sharp telson, and rear limbs modified into paddles, *Pterygotus* was probably the best swimmer among the sea scorpions.

Eurypterus (you-RIP-ter-us) was a more modestly sized sea scorpion that survived into the Permian period, 250 million years ago. Perhaps the most common of all the sea scorpions, *Eurypterus* was a swimmer with large paddles. Its chelicerae were so short that they did not reach past the edge of its head shield.

MIXOPTERUS (extinct)

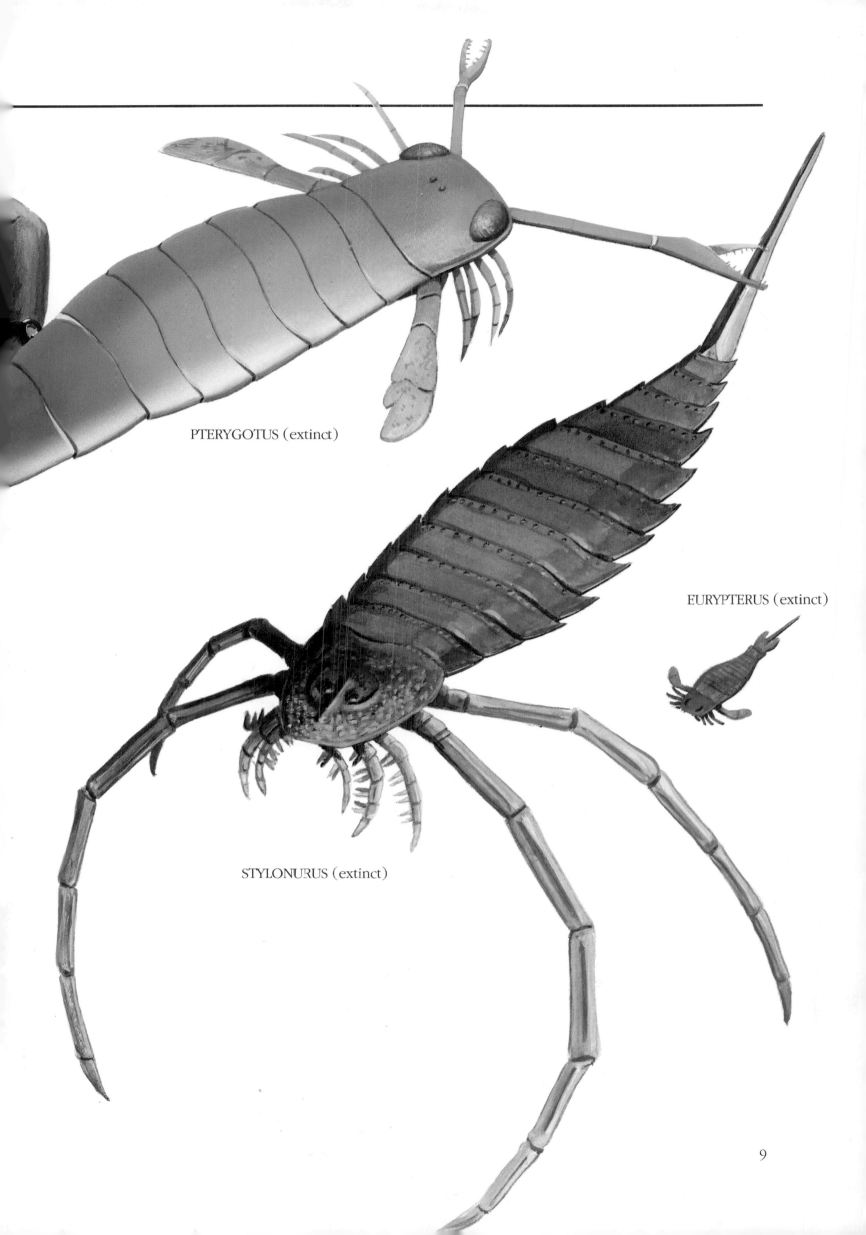

PTERYGOTUS (extinct)

EURYPTERUS (extinct)

STYLONURUS (extinct)

9

Ponderous Placoderms

Placoderms (PLAK-oh-dermz) (meaning "plate-skinned") are extinct fish that were unlike any living today. Their armorlike skeletons usually covered only the head, trunk, and jaws, while the tail and fins remained uncovered. Most placoderms were small, less than two feet in length. They lived during the Devonian period, 400 to 350 million years ago.

Placoderms started out as bottom feeders. Only a few made the transition to open-water feeding. Placoderms did not have teeth. Instead, the sharp bones of the jaw served the same purpose.

Dunkleosteus (dun-kul-AH-stee-us) was the great white shark of its day and grew to twenty feet in length. This predator's jaws were powerful, and its bite must have sliced its victims in two. Like a snapping turtle, *Dunkleosteus* may have rested on its flat chest armor between meals. Fossils of this placoderm have been found in eastern North America, Europe, and North Africa, which were underwater portions of one supercontinent at the time.

A relative, *Gorgonichthys* (gore-gon-IK-theez), named for the Gorgons of mythology, had huge eyes and fanglike "teeth." It was found in eastern North America.

With a skull measuring three feet in length, *Titanichthys* (tye-tan-IK-theez) was the largest animal of its day. This placoderm's skull and trunk shields were very wide and low, resembling a turtle's shell. *Titanichthys* may have been a mud shoveler, scooping mouthfuls of seafloor into its jaws and filtering out edible items. Fossils of this placoderm have been found in North America, Africa, and eastern Europe.

Bothriolepis (bahth-ree-oh-LEEP-iss) lived in the fresh waters of eastern Canada. With its armored fins it plowed through ooze up to its eyes, vacuuming up worms and other tiny animals.

Flattened *Gemuendina* (gem-wen-DEEN-ah) had huge pectoral fins that made it look like a ray or an angel shark. With eyes that stared straight up, this rare European placoderm probably buried itself in sand until it was ready to feed.

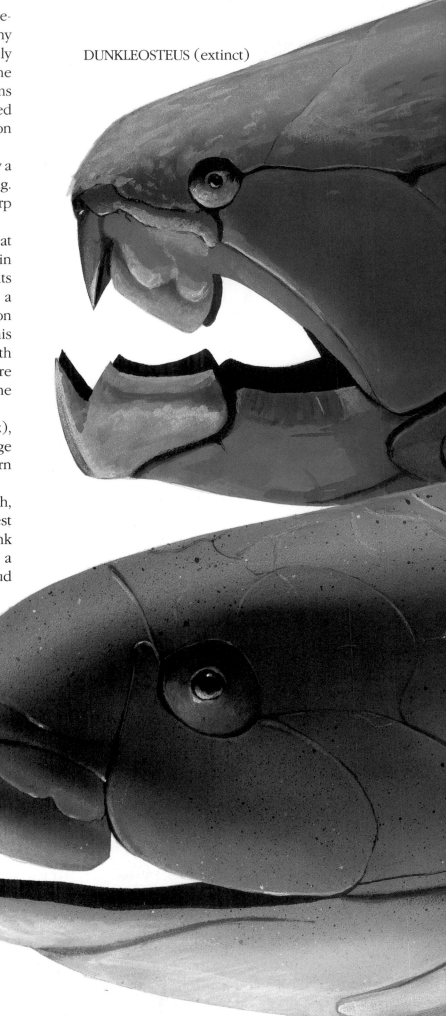

DUNKLEOSTEUS (extinct)

TITANICHTHYS (extinct)

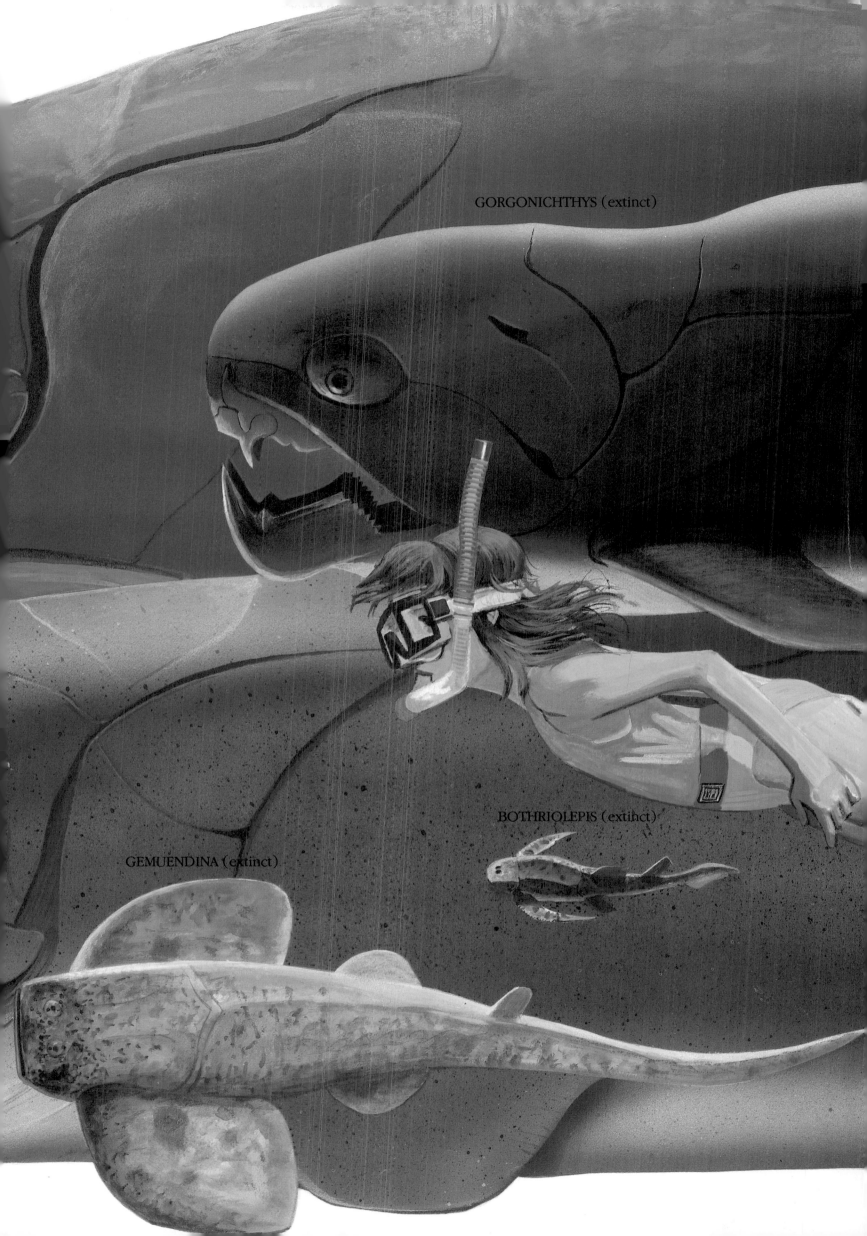

GORGONICHTHYS (extinct)

BOTHRIOLEPIS (extinct)

GEMUENDINA (extinct)

Strange Sharks

Sharks are fish with a skeleton made of cartilage, not bone. Bone *is* found in shark scales, however, which are shaped like tiny teeth and feel like sandpaper. Sharks have no gill covers; instead, each of their gills opens directly to the outside.

The *goblin shark* was first known as a seventy-million-year-old fossil, which was named in the 1880s. A living example was not discovered until ten years later.

Also called the elfin shark, the goblin has an outrageous shovel-shaped snout, which it apparently uses to dig up the seabed while looking for food. Like so many deep-water species, the goblin has small fins and a long, flexible tail. Instead of having an underslung mouth like many other sharks, this one has a protruding snout, which can be extended even farther when feeding. The teeth of the goblin shark are needle shaped and very long. Some of the upper teeth are large enough to overlap the lower jaw when the goblin closes its mouth.

Only a few specimens of the goblin shark have ever been caught. They are rarely seen because they live in the deep seas. So far the catches have been in waters near Japan, Australia, and Portugal, indicating that the goblin shark probably swims all the world's oceans.

Wobbegong (WOB-bee-gong) is the aboriginal name of a carpet shark found among reef hollows and caves in shallow tropical Australian seas. Carpet sharks, as their name implies, are flat, and they rest on the seafloor by day. They rise to forage only after dark. The patchy wobbegong shark blends in well with its surroundings. Often it lies half-buried in sand. Fleshy skin tassles around its mouth act as camouflage because they resemble algae or seaweeds.

Carpet sharks are very different from their better-known open-sea cousins. Their tails do not turn up but are in line with the rest of the body.

The wobbegong's mouth is wide—almost straight—and it opens at the tip of its snout rather than beneath it. For a shark, the wobbegong's teeth are small. Despite being quite sluggish, the wobbegong occasionally stirs to catch passing fish, crabs, sea urchins, or squid, and sometimes it will scavenge a carcass.

Unlike most other sharks, the wobbegong does not have to keep swimming in order to keep fresh water circulating through its gills. In fact, it doesn't even have to open its mouth. Water enters this shark through spiracles, small openings behind each eye, which remain above the surface of the seafloor when the shark is half-buried.

The fossils of small carpet sharks have been

HELIOCOPRION (extinct)

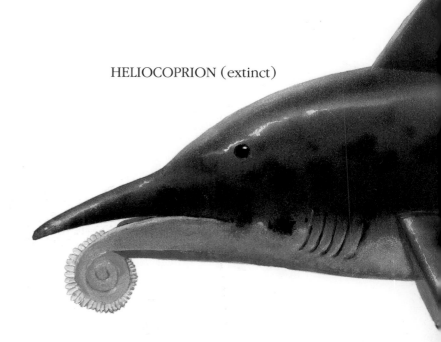

WOBBEGONG

identified from as far back as the Jurassic period, approximately 190 million years ago.

No one really knows for sure what *Heliocoprion* (hee-lee-oh-COPE-ree-on) looked like. All that remains of this extinct shark is a very peculiar set of teeth. As this shark grew it did not shed its baby teeth. Instead the teeth accumulated in a spiral at the tip of its lower jaw. In related fossil sharks, the teeth on either side of this tooth spiral were flattened for crushing hard-shelled animals, such as crabs and molluscs.

The body attached to the teeth illustrated here is taken from the closest known relative of *Heliocoprion*. This relative was a fairly normal-looking shark except that it had a symmetrical tail fin, no anal fin, no second dorsal fin, and no pelvic fins. It also had a long snout projecting above its tooth whorl. *Heliocoprion* lived 270 million years ago, during the early Permian period, and its fossils are found worldwide.

Fabulous Fish

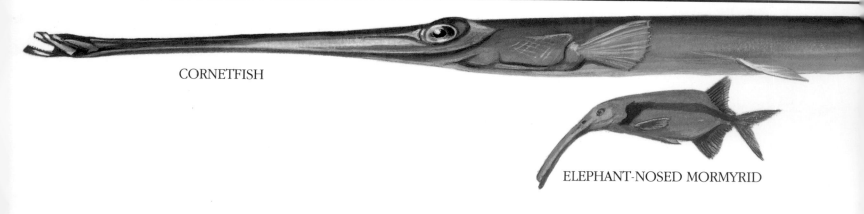

CORNETFISH

ELEPHANT-NOSED MORMYRID

Imagine a fish reaching six feet in length but weighing only 7½ pounds. That's the *cornetfish,* or flutemouth—a giant pipefish. With its extremely long, tubular mouth, the cornetfish can suck in any small swimming organism. Unique among pipefish, the cornetfish has a long filament extending from the middle of its tail. Common in tropical seas, cornetfish sometimes swim in loose schools. (See pages 20–21 for more about other pipefish.)

The *elephant-nosed mormyrid* (more-MYE-rid) has a long, curved, inflexible snout that acts as a probe. Living in the murky waters of African lakes and rivers, mormyrids feed on insects, worms and other bottom dwellers. This fish is capable of finding larvae in the smallest crevices because touching and tasting occur at the tip of its special snout. Fine control in tight places is handled by the paired dorsal and anal fins, which are able to propel the elephant-nosed mormyrid forward and backward with equal ease. Usually it is active only after dark.

The elephant-nosed mormyrid may also find its prey with an electric field generated by its own muscles. This field acts like radar. When some object enters the field, a disruption occurs, which the mormyrid's giant brain can sense and interpret. Mormyrids have the largest brain weight to body weight ratio of any fish: 2:100, which is the same as it is in humans.

The *fanfish* is a rare species that lives at moderate depths in southern oceans. This silvery fish has huge blue dorsal and anal fins. What use they are, except possibly as decoration, remains unknown. This fish's waste and egg opening has been shifted so far forward by the size of its extra-large lower fin that the fanfish lays eggs from beneath its chin.

In mythology the Chimaera (ky-MEER-uh) is a monster with the body parts of other animals. The living *chimaeras,* otherwise known as ratfish and sea rats, were once thought to have been part bony fish and part shark. Chimaeras are actually very strange sharks. They have a skeleton made of cartilage, and they lay their large eggs in horny capsules. Whereas a shark's jaws

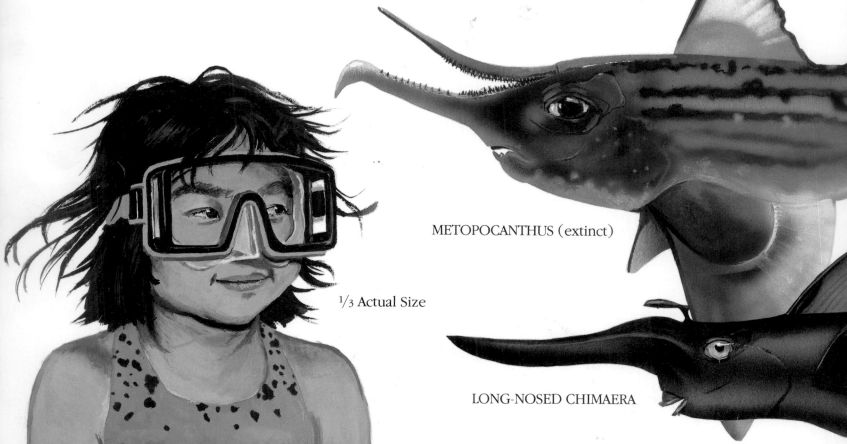

¹/₃ Actual Size

METOPOCANTHUS (extinct)

LONG-NOSED CHIMAERA

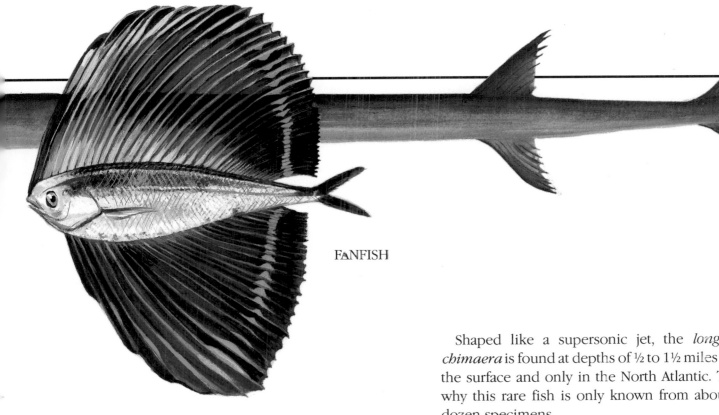

FANFISH

Shaped like a supersonic jet, the *long-nosed chimaera* is found at depths of ½ to 1½ miles below the surface and only in the North Atlantic. That is why this rare fish is only known from about one dozen specimens.

Metopocanthus (met-uh-poe-KANTH-us) had a huge clasper barbed with many sharp teeth. This clasper must have looked like another set of jaws. *Metopocanthus*, also a chimaera, lived in what is now England during the Jurassic period, 180 million years ago.

Iniopteryx (in-ee-OP-ter-iks) was considered a chimaera cousin, but it must have been a distant one. The pectoral fins were the craziest thing about this unique fish. They were positioned near the nape of its neck, and they moved up and down, almost like the wings of a bird. These fins were very thick and bore a series of hooks along their leading edges. Perhaps the hooks acted like chimaera claspers. *Iniopteryx* had a large head, a stocky body, gill covers, and a round tail. Unlike a chimaera, its jaws contained many delicate teeth and were not fused to its braincase. *Iniopteryx* lived in North America during the late Carboniferous period, 300 million years ago.

are free to move independently of its skull, a chimaera's jaw is fused to its braincase. Chimaeras are also unlike sharks because they have gill covers, and male chimaeras have unusual claspers on top of their head. Because chimaeras fertilize internally, the claspers are probably used to maintain position during mating. Chimaeras defend themselves with the long spine that supports their dorsal fin. This spine has a poison gland at its base, making the chimaera a dangerous fish to bother.

Chimaeras have unusual teeth, shaped like plates, which are built for crushing. They eat molluscs, starfish, and small seafloor fish. Chimaeras swim by flapping their large pectoral fins. Their long, whip-like tails trail almost uselessly behind. Chimaeras are ancient fish, virtually unchanged since the Carboniferous period, 350 million years ago.

INIOPTERYX (extinct)

Amazing Anglerfish

Unlike most fish, anglerfish are not speedy or streamlined. They don't need to chase their food. "Anglers" are so named because they fish for other fish by using "bait" on the end of a "line." The fishing "lure" of an anglerfish is actually a part of its own body. The fleshy bait and the "rod" it hangs from are highly modified and movable portions of a spine from the dorsal fin. Like human fishermen, anglerfish remain very still while fishing to avoid frightening their prey. Only their lures wriggle, enticing small fish to come within striking distance.

There are basically two kinds of anglers, bottom dwellers, which live in shallow waters, and deep-sea anglers.

In total darkness, deep-sea anglers rely on luminous bait to attract their prey. The female deep-sea anglers have a fishing organ, and it is unique to each species; the males do not. The glow of the lure is probably created by luminous bacteria. Food is scarce in the deep oceans, so anglers can't be choosy. Some are able to feed on fish larger than themselves. That's why most deep-sea anglers have such a big mouth and a stretchable stomach.

In general, deep-sea anglerfish are surprisingly small. The males of each species are smaller than the females. Most males have given up even acting like fish and have become parasites. One or more can cling to a female, nourished by her blood-stream. Males have their own gill systems for oxygen, but food is supplied by their female host. This parasitic relationship makes sure a male is nearby when the eggs need to be fertilized.

The fertilized eggs of deep-sea anglers float to the surface, where the young develop and feed on plankton. At the surface they find mates before descending to the depths.

Deep-sea anglers are found in the warmer waters of all the world's oceans, usually at depths of 1,000 to 13,000 feet. The small gill opening of deep-sea anglers is hidden in an unusual place, *behind* each pectoral fin.

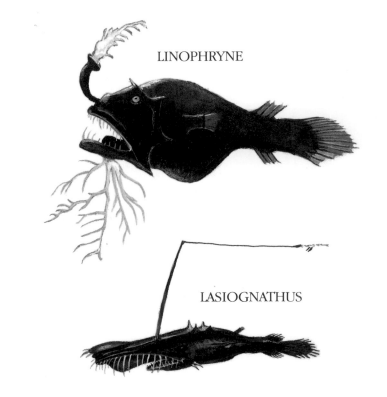

LINOPHRYNE

LASIOGNATHUS

CAULOPHRYNE

BATFISH

Linophryne (line-uh-FRY-nee) is all head and belly. Its lure is shaped like an Olympic torch and its touch-sensitive chin whiskers resemble branching roots.

Caulophryne (kall-uh-FRY-nee) has been found at depths of 33 to 5,000 feet. The female has huge dorsal and anal fin rays. Sharp teeth fill its mouth. Males have a hook in each jawbone. Together the hooks act as pincers to hold the male in place on the female. *Caulophryne* eats fish, squid, and swimming crustaceans, such as shrimp.

Lasiognathus (lass-ee-OG-nath-us) is one of the rarest of all fish. Only a few specimens have ever been caught. *Lasiognathus* is less rotund than other deep-sea anglers, but it has a rod, a line, and a lure. Its lure is not only luminous but hooked in three places. The rod may point forward, like a lance, or be raised erect, like a periscope. This angler's upper jaw extends far beyond its lower. When the upper jaw is raised, a vacuum forms, which sweeps anything nearby into the mouth.

Far from the ocean's depths, *frogfish* are camouflaged "sit-and-wait" anglers that live in shallow sunlit waters. They move only rarely, but when they do they walk or hop on their fins.

There are many kinds of frogfish, and each one is able to change its color to match its surroundings. The change is often slow, taking up to a month. Some frogfish may be mistaken for a piece of bumpy coral on which to lay eggs, graze, or seek shelter.

Each type of frogfish has its own special lure. Some lures resemble worms. The lure of the *warty frogfish* resembles a small fish. Small fish may attack the lure as if it were a rival. The frogfish can extend its mouth and engulf its victim in six milliseconds—faster than any other known vertebrate.

Batfish are flattened anglers that charge across the seafloor like tanks. With their large pectoral fins, small supportive pelvic fins, and round gill openings that open to the rear, they resemble stealth bombers.

The fishing organ of a batfish is enclosed in a tube and emerges from a nostrillike pit directly above the mouth. Tipped with a wormlike lure, it can be extended, retracted, and twitched to attract a meal.

Most batfish are less than six inches in length. The largest grow to fourteen inches. Only one, a comical batfish found near the Galápagos Islands, is decorated with humanlike lips that seem to be painted in lipstick.

WARTY FROGFISH

Actual size

BLACK SWALLOWER

Devilish Deep-Sea Fish

Deep-sea fish are often quite unlike those found near the surface. They are specially adapted to lack of light, frigid waters, tremendous pressure, and a scarcity of food. Some fish have been discovered on the floors of the deepest oceans, nearly seven miles below the surface.

The slippery *black swallower,* a distant relative of eels, lives 1.2 to 3 miles below the surface. Some swallowers reach 5½ feet in length, with a tapering tail that can be tipped with branching filaments and light organs. Other fish may be attracted to these lights. If they are, this velvety black predator may merely have to turn in a tight circle to find its next meal chasing its tail. The black swallower's stomach can expand to accommodate prey even larger than itself.

The *viperfish* was named for its enormous viperlike fangs. These fangs are so large that they protrude in bulldog fashion whenever this fish shuts its mouth. This twelve-inch-long predator prowls midocean depths. Two rows of light organs illuminate the viperfish's lower side—perhaps to attract potential mates.

Gigantura (jye-gan-TOOR-ah) has twin telescopes for eyes. They are said to be among the most sensitive eyes in the animal kingdom. Most fish have eyes on the sides of the head, giving them a wide field of view. *Gigantura*'s eyes face directly forward, the way human eyes do, giving this fish excellent depth perception. Found in very deep tropical waters, the scaleless *Gigantura* grows to six inches in length, including the large lower tail fin for which it is named. Its butterflylike pectoral fins fan water into its gills when *Gigantura*'s mouth is stuffed with prey.

Malacosteus (mal-uh-KOSS-tee-us) has jaws that are longer than its skull. Not many fish are too large for this jet black terror of the deep. Although *Malacosteus* is almost ten inches long, it has only a tiny tail. Instead, the dorsal and anal fins are extra large and act like a tail. A light organ shines beneath each eye of *Malacosteus*—possibly to attract and illuminate potential prey.

The *ribbon sawtail fish* is so incredibly stretched out that it looks as if it is made of taffy. Growing to as much as fifteen inches in length, this scaleless dragon of the deep is a fierce predator. Only females have teeth; the males are toothless. The ribbon sawtail fish has no pectoral fins as an adult. In addition, males lose their pelvic fins. They swim like snakes through the inky water. A touch-sensitive chin barbel helps the ribbon sawtail fish

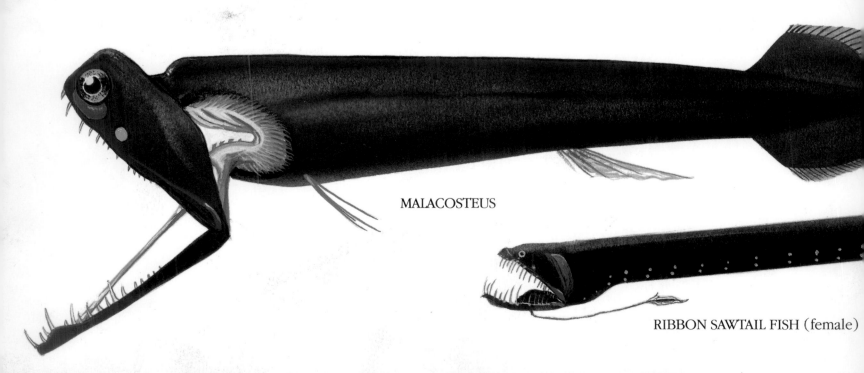

MALACOSTEUS

RIBBON SAWTAIL FISH (female)

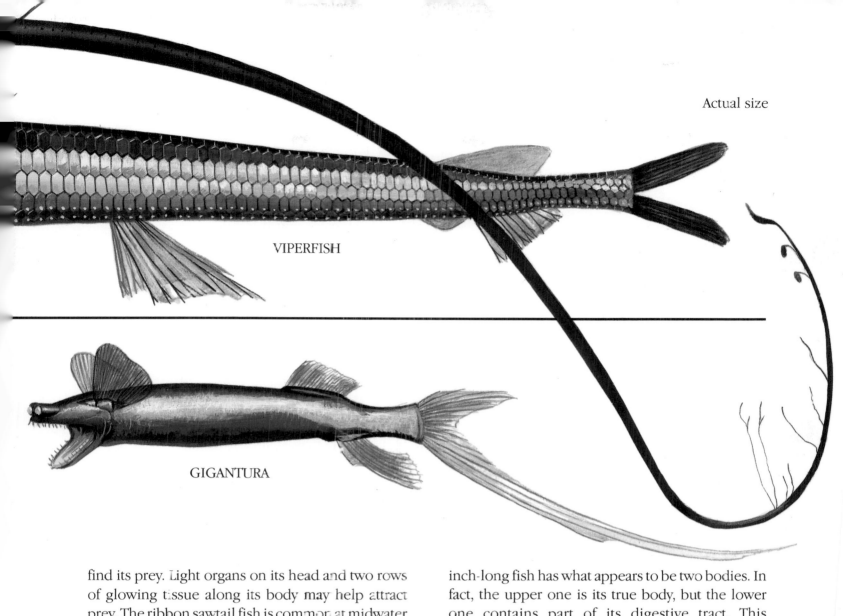

VIPERFISH

GIGANTURA

find its prey. Light organs on its head and two rows of glowing tissue along its body may help attract prey. The ribbon sawtail fish is common at midwater depths in all tropical waters.

The larva of the *ribbon sawtail fish* has the most unusual eyes of all. These eyes dangle at the end of long stalks that sometimes become knotted as the larva grows into an adult.

The larvae of many fish bear little resemblance to their parents, but the larva known as *Exterilium* (eks-ter-ILL-ee-um) may be the strangest of all. Known from a single specimen, this 2¾-

inch-long fish has what appears to be two bodies. In fact, the upper one is its true body, but the lower one contains part of its digestive tract. This appendage may serve as a flotation device, and its white streamers may mimic the stinging tentacles of a jellyfish.

The *tripod fish* walks on the floor of the ocean on the tips of its long, sensitive fin rays. The seafloor is deep with ooze in many places, and these fin rays act as feelers. They can probably distinguish organisms from sediment.

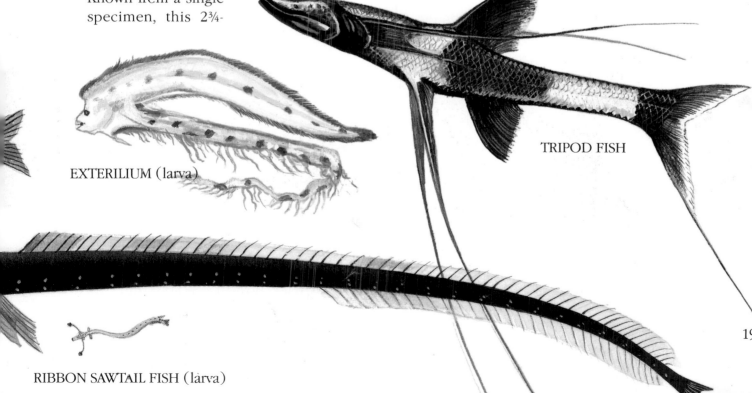

EXTERILIUM (larva)

TRIPOD FISH

RIBBON SAWTAIL FISH (larva)

LEAFY SEA DRAGON

Spectacular Sea Dragons & Their Relatives

Pipefish, sea horses, and sea dragons are among the most unfishlike of fishes. Instead of jaws, these fish have a long tube through which they siphon their tiny prey. Instead of shiny scales, they are protected by an armor of bony plates. Instead of giving birth or laying eggs, females stand by as the males produce young. Instead of having a streamlined shape, sea horses and sea dragons have a neck, a head that bends at a right angle to the body, and a tail that contributes almost nothing to their forward progress.

Pipefish most closely resemble the ancestral tube-mouth fish from which the others are derived. A pipefish looks like a long, stretched-out traditional fish. Ranging from one to eighteen inches in

length, pipefish, like all tube mouths, live close to shore in waters less than 500 feet deep. It does not have a prehensile tail, and its eggs are carried in the open, not in a brood pouch.

The remarkable *sea horse* has a tail that is more prehensile than an elephant's trunk. Mostly it is used to hang on to coral and sea grass. The sea horse swims by undulating its transparent dorsal and pectoral fins. It turns by first twisting its head in the direction it wants to go. Sea horses eat a lot and grow fast. They feed on brine shrimp and other tiny floating organisms.

The *leafy sea dragon* of southern Australian waters may look like a sea horse gone wild, but

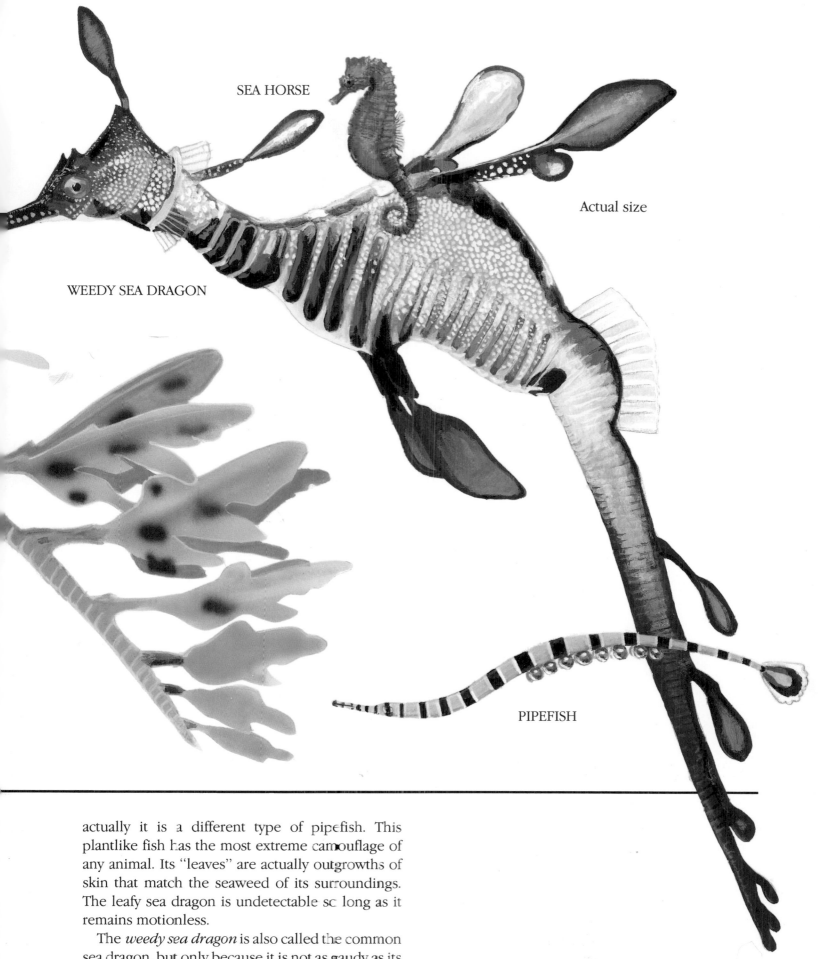

SEA HORSE

Actual size

WEEDY SEA DRAGON

PIPEFISH

actually it is a different type of pipefish. This plantlike fish has the most extreme camouflage of any animal. Its "leaves" are actually outgrowths of skin that match the seaweed of its surroundings. The leafy sea dragon is undetectable so long as it remains motionless.

The *weedy sea dragon* is also called the common sea dragon, but only because it is not as gaudy as its cousin. The weedy sea dragon lives in kelp forests south of Australia and grows to twelve inches in length. The male may carry as many as 120 pink eggs beneath its tail. It moves slowly, if at all, waiting for the currents to bring microorganisms within reach of its vacuum-cleaner snout.

Incredible Insects

Many insects are called bugs, but in order to be considered a *true* bug an insect must have piercing and sucking mouth parts. True bugs suck plant sap. *Treehoppers* are true bugs. An enlargement of their middle body section (thorax) extends back over their abdomen. Horns, knobs, and antlers make some treehoppers hard for animals to swallow, but they especially make them hard to spot. Most treehoppers are disguised to resemble thorns or other tiny pieces of plants. Treehoppers are tiny, and these ornaments are hollow, so they do not weigh very much. Treehoppers live almost anywhere, from the jungles of the Amazon to the heights of the Himalaya Mountains.

Treehoppers don't actually hop much, except in an emergency. They don't fly much either. All day long they just suck plant sap. Maple syrup is a plant sap that humans enjoy. What a treehopper sucks is also very sweet. Some of this sweetness passes through the bug's digestive system. Its anus may be "milked" by hungry ants.

Beetles are the most common of all insects. Their front wings form hard covers for their flying wings. They have mouth parts for chewing and gnawing. Beetles find mates primarily by smelling their perfume with their antennae, which are often elaborate.

Weevils are beetles with a long snout from which their antennae extend. The *giraffe beetle* is a weevil with an extraordinarily long and bizarre head, which is held aloft. Less than an inch high, the giraffe beetle is found in Madagascar.

The smallest of insects, *fairy flies*, are wasps that weigh less than some one-celled animals. They grow to less than two-tenths of a millimeter in length. The front wings of a fairy fly are simply a single wing vein fringed with tiny hairs. The hind wings are as slender as its legs. Fairy flies are parasites of other insects' eggs.

The *stalk-eyed fly* uses its eyes to measure up rivals in territorial contests. Even its tiny antennae have migrated out on the eye stalks. Stalk-eyed flies live in Africa, where their larvae (maggots) attack cornstalks.

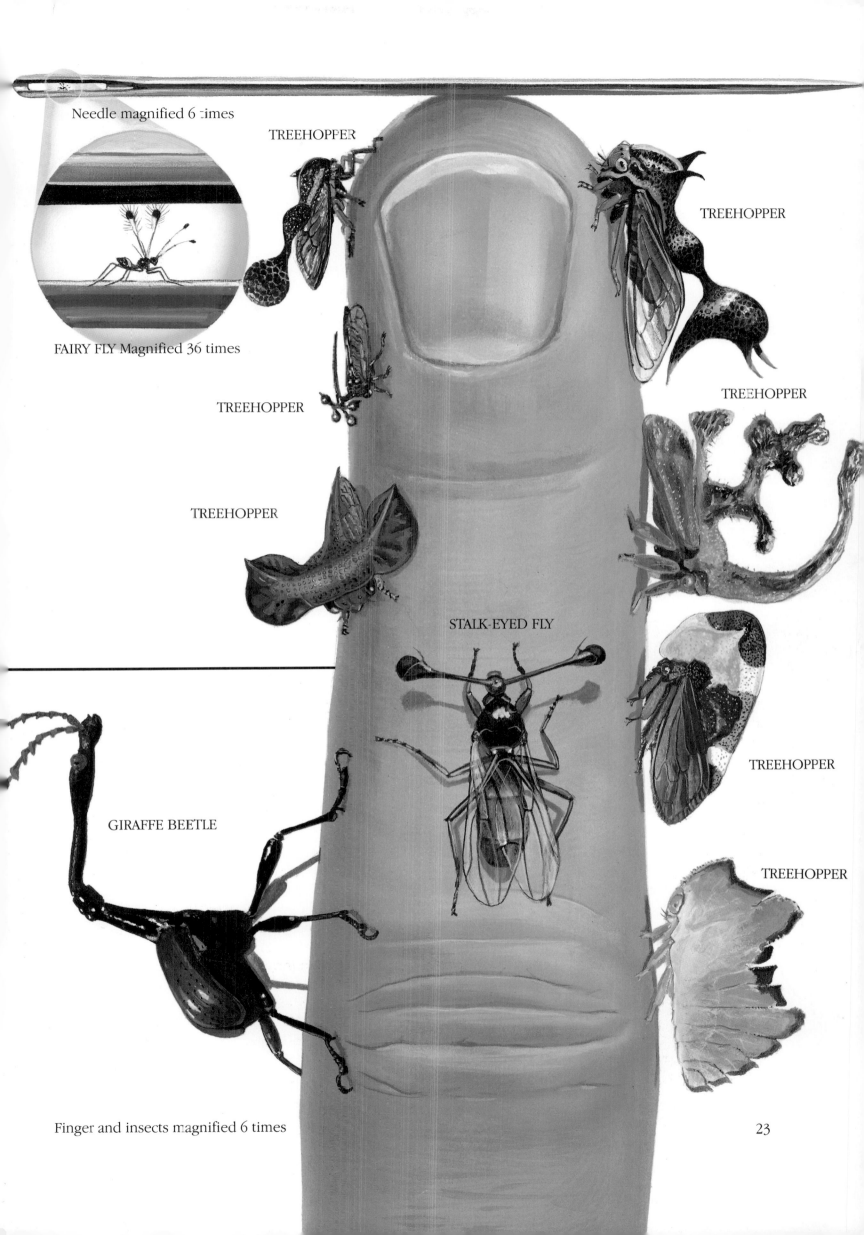

Needle magnified 6 times

TREEHOPPER

TREEHOPPER

FAIRY FLY Magnified 36 times

TREEHOPPER

TREEHOPPER

TREEHOPPER

STALK-EYED FLY

TREEHOPPER

GIRAFFE BEETLE

TREEHOPPER

Finger and insects magnified 6 times

23

Awesome Amphibians

Amphibians are anatomical intermediates between fish and reptiles. Like fish, they lay unshelled eggs and, while they are still tadpoles, extract oxygen from water through their gills. Like reptiles, most adult amphibians have four legs and breathe air. Today amphibians have naked skin, but in the past most amphibians were armored with bony scales, or scutes. Such scales did not prevent amphibians from drying out, so these creatures spent much of their time in or near water.

Amphibians rest on their bellies, rising to move only for short periods of time. Their legs sprawl out to the sides and in many cases are too short to enable them to raise their bellies off the ground.

Eupelor (YOU-pe-lore) had the flattest head of any amphibian, perhaps the flattest in the animal kingdom. It probably waited on the lake bottom, watching prey swimming just above its head. When

it was hungry it would quickly open its mouth, sucking the fish into the vacuum created within its jaws. Rather than dropping its lower jaw, which would have been lying flat on the bottom of the lake, *Eupelor* had to raise its head. If the water was darkened, *Eupelor* could still sense its prey with the lateral-line canals on its head. Lateral-line canals are sensitive to minute underwater disturbances. *Eupelor* probably never left the water but rose occasionally to the surface for a breath. Like many other flat-headed amphibians, *Eupelor* lived in Texas during the late Triassic period, close to the area now known as the Petrified Forest.

Plagiosternum (plah-jee-oh-STER-num) was another flat-headed amphibian. It was only distantly related to *Eupelor*. Its head was wider than it was long, yet it too fed by quickly raising its head underwater to suck in prey. The muscles that opened its

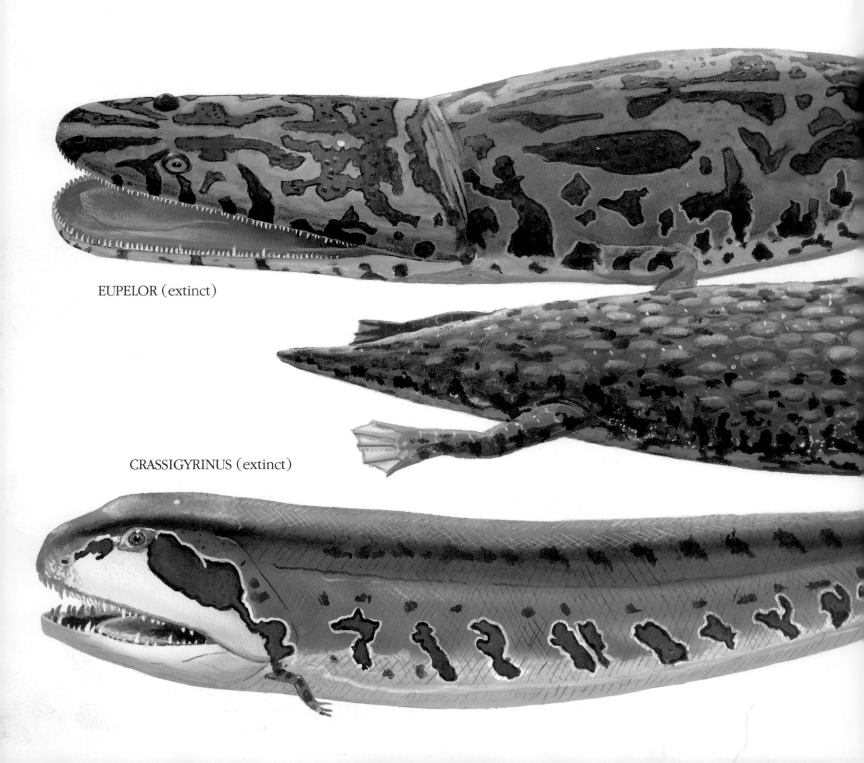

EUPELOR (extinct)

CRASSIGYRINUS (extinct)

jaw were very strong, and those that closed its jaw were weak. Huge eyes topped this "sit-and-wait" predator's skull. *Plagiosternum* lacked a special notch at the rear of its skull, which most amphibians have. Some breathed through a hole there. Others had an eardrum stretched across this notch. As an underwater animal, *Plagiosternum* had little need for either. This amphibian lived during the Middle Triassic period in tropical Spitzbergen, an island which is north of the Arctic Circle today.

Diploceraspis (dip-loe-ser-ASS-pis) was another flat-headed amphibian unrelated to the other two. It was the most outlandish of the "boomerang heads" and lived in what is now Ohio during the early Permian period, 270 million years ago. *Diploceraspis* did not have as huge a mouth as other amphibians, but its cheekbones were greatly expanded to form horns. Most likely these horns

were used in duels. They would have also made *Diploceraspis* more difficult to swallow.

Prionosuchus (pree-oh-nuh-SOOK-us) was also a fish eater, but it did not rely on sucking fish into its mouth. Instead, its jaws were long and narrow and could move quickly through the water to snap at prey. It looked like a crocodile or a gavial and probably had similar habits. Like most aquatic amphibians, it had lateral lines all over its skull. Only the snout and a few other bones are known of this rare Brazilian amphibian from the early Permian period.

Crassigyrinus (kras-see-jye-RYE-nus) was a very primitive and unusual amphibian whose ancestors evidently returned to an aquatic life shortly after getting legs. This swimmer's limbs were tiny and almost useless. *Crassigyrinus* is known from two specimens; one is a complete skeleton that is missing only the tail and parts of the hind limbs. This underwater predator had a large head, with deep cheeks, and a weak backbone, almost like a fish's. Small teeth lined its jaws and large fangs descended from the roof of its mouth. *Crassigyrinus* lived during the late Carboniferous period in tropical Scotland.

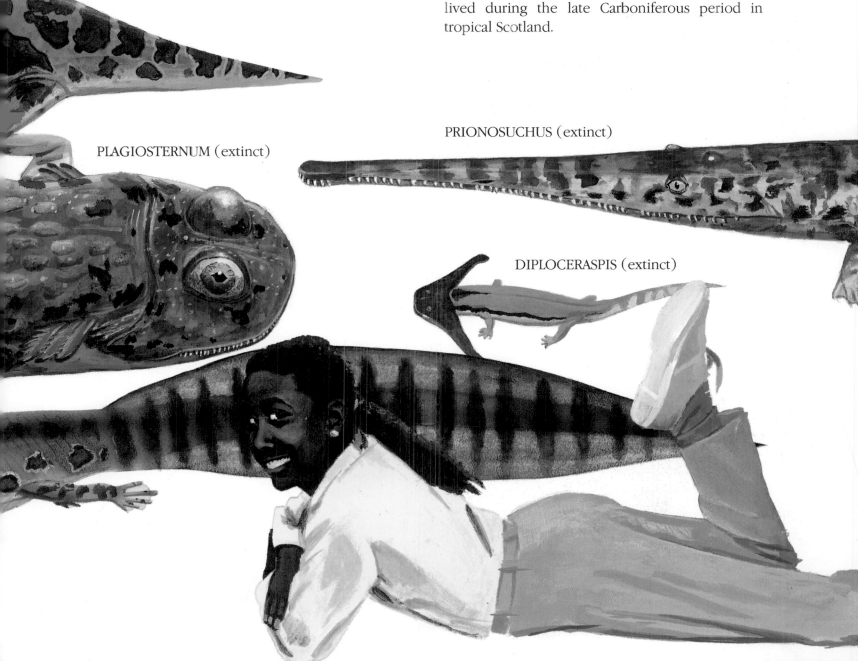

PLAGIOSTERNUM (extinct)

PRIONOSUCHUS (extinct)

DIPLOCERASPIS (extinct)

Legendary Lizards

Chameleons are the most unusual of all living lizards. Their sticky tongues can stretch to an incredible length to snare prey. Their tails coil around branches. Their "hands" are divided between the third and fourth "fingers," and their feet are divided between the second and third toes, for getting a better grip on branches. Chameleons "disappear" into their surroundings by changing color and by moving very slowly. A chameleon's eyes move independently of each other beneath armored eyelids until they lock on a target.

Adding to its bizarre appearance, the *three-horned Jackson's chameleon* has horns to intimidate rivals and excite potential mates. Today chameleons are found mostly in southern Asia and in Africa south of the Sahara.

Drepanosaurus (dre-PAN-uh-sore-us) was an unusual lizard of the late Triassic period (210 million years ago) in Italy. It had stong claws on its front and hind limbs, but the claw on the second digit of its "hands" was huge! The tail of this nineteen-inch-long digger was powerful and ended with a peculiar hook at its tip. Perhaps this hook was used as some sort of anchor. No one knows what the head of *Drepanosaurus* looked like because it is missing from the fossil.

Gaudy Gliders

Sharovipteryx (shar-ov-IP-ter-iks) was a lizardlike tree dweller that lived in Russia during the early Triassic period, 240 million years ago. It glided with a wing membrane stretched behind its long, thin hind legs. A small membrane may also have extended behind each tiny arm. This may seem backward, but a number of modern jets employ a similar wing design. *Sharovipteryx* lived in a desert area dotted with salt lakes and conifer trees.

Icarosaurus (IK-uh-roe-sore-us) was named after Icarus, the mythological figure who flew too close to the sun on wings made of feathers and wax. A resident of the jungles of New Jersey during the late Triassic period, this near lizard had tremendously elongated ribs, which supported a durable wing membrane. Jointed at their base, these ribs folded back alongside the body when the wings were not outstretched. *Icarosaurus* could have glided more than one hundred feet at a time. It would also have displayed its brightly colored rib membranes during courtship.

THREE-HORNED JACKSON'S CHAMELEON

DREPANOSAURUS (extinct)

SHAROVIPTERYX (extinct)

ICAROSAURUS (extinct)

Actual size

Peculiar Placodonts

Placodont (PLAK-uh-dont) means "plate toothed." Instead of having spiky teeth, as most reptiles do, placodonts had unusual flat teeth, which they used to crush hard-shelled crustaceans, oysters, and clams. Placodonts are distantly related to archosaurs (AR-ko-sorz), the ancestors of dinosaurs and crocodiles, and nothosaurs (NO-thuh-sorz), otter-like swimming reptiles. Not many specimens of placodonts are known, but they all seem to have had some sort of bony armor. Placodonts lived only during the Triassic period, a time spanning thirty-five million years. They swam in the shallow coastal waters of a sea that once existed between Eurasia and Africa/Arabia.

Henodus (HEN-uh-dus) lived during the late Triassic period in Germany. It looked like a turtle but was not one. The upper shell was supported by a framework of long ribs roofed over by bony hexagons and horny diamond-shaped scales. No layer of bony plates protected the many belly ribs. Protected by its broad, flat shell, *Henodus* may have buried itself in sand to avoid detection. *Henodus* had only four flat teeth and strainer plates along the edge of its squared-off beak. These strainers would have trapped tiny floating sea creatures that drifted by in the surf.

Placochelys (plak-uh-KEEL-eez), or "plated turtle," looked like a sea turtle but was not one. *Placochelys* had limbs transformed into swimming paddles and probably swam like a sea turtle. Perhaps it also came ashore at night on certain deserted beaches to lay its eggs. Like all placodonts, *Placochelys* had strong jaw muscles and crushing tooth plates in its palate, but unlike others it had a narrow, toothless snout.

PLACOCHELYS (extinct)

TANYSTROPHEUS (extinct)

HENODUS (extinct)

28

Tremendous Tanystropheus

Another resident of the Triassic sea that once covered Germany and Switzerland was *Tanystropheus* (tan-ee-STROFE-ee-us), which means "long vertebrae." No animal of its size had a longer or stiffer neck. Its neck had only twelve vertebrae. The long, springy ribs on both sides of each neck bone helped the neck act like a fiberglass fishing rod, snapping the neck back after each strike.

Tanystropheus was a protorosaur, related most closely to archosaurs. Adults had long, pointed teeth for snaring large fish. Young ones had three-pronged teeth better for catching tiny prey.

A Radical Rhynchosaur

Rhynchosaurs (RINE-koe-sorz), or "beaked lizards," are little-known plant-eating reptiles that were common and widespread during the Triassic period. *Hyperodapedon* (hye-per-uh-DAP-eh-don) was a four-foot-long rhynchosaur that had very bizarre teeth. Most reptiles shed their teeth continually, replacing old, worn teeth with new, sharp ones. *Hyperodapedon* had flat teeth with long, curved roots. As in modern rodents, these teeth continued to grow and wear away as long as the animal lived.

Powering these mighty choppers were such huge jaw muscles that *Hyperodapedon*'s skull was wider than it was long. *Hyperodapedon* also had a peculiar beak. Two bony prongs of the upper jaw formed the upper beak, with a single nostril opening between them. Two bony prongs of the lower jaw formed the lower beak. Together the beak sections acted like pruning shears to snip twigs and roots in half.

HYPERODAPEDON (extinct)

Creepy Crocodiles

GEOSAURUS (extinct)

A crocodile's skull is massive and solid, rather than lightweight and flexible. This helps the crocodile withstand the stress of biting large animals. Unlike that of any other reptile, the roof of a crocodile's skull overhangs its temple regions, the way the roof of a house overhangs its walls. Finally, most crocodiles are armored with scutes along their necks, backs, and tails. Scutes are squarish skin bones, which interlock to form a stiff girdle that prevents side-to-side undulations and helps crocodiles keep their bellies from dragging while they walk.

The earliest known crocodilian, *Gracilisuchus* (gra-seel-i-SOOK-us), or "slender crocodile," looked more like a primitive dinosaur because it walked on its hind legs alone. *Gracilisuchus* used its huge eyes to spot lizards in the underbrush, and its long legs to chase them to exhaustion. Scutes were very important because they kept this crocodilian from wobbling too much while running. *Gracilisuchus* lived in Argentina during the middle Triassic

period, 220 million years ago, alongside the first mammals and dinosaurs.

Terristrisuchus (ter-riss-tri-SOOK-us), or "earth crocodile," was the most delicately built and long-legged of all the crocodilians. *Terristrisuchus* looked more like a scaly greyhound than the crocodiles that live today. Perhaps this predator sprinted over the uplands of Great Britain (where its fossils were discovered), coming to water only to drink. This crocodile had erect limbs, like those of a dinosaur, rather than sprawling ones. Evidently sprinting crocodiles were no match for their more famous cousins, because they became extinct following the invasion of the dinosaurs during the late Triassic period 200 million years ago.

Other than penguins, the only archosaurs to become highly adapted to life in the water were sea crocodiles such as *Geosaurus* (JEE-oh-sore-us), or "earth lizard." "Sea crocs" existed throughout the Jurassic period and the first part of the Cretaceous period. Most of their fossils come from Europe, but

BAURUSUCHUS (extinct)

GRACILISUCHUS (extinct)

a few are known from North and South America. *Geosaurus* had short paddles for forelimbs and small but typically shaped hind limbs. Perhaps it needed legs in order to lay eggs on land the way living crocodiles do. *Geosaurus*'s tail bent down to support a sharklike tail fin. Like most marine animals, *Geosaurus* had a shortened neck, giving it less flexibility there, but a large number of back vertebrae, providing increased flexibility. Unlike other crocodiles, streamlined sea crocs had no scutes. In addition, they had no scales, which helped them slip more easily through the water. Instead of having eyeballs on top of their skulls, sea crocs had eyes on the sides, protected by a bone that shaded their eyes from glare, giving them a permanent "eagle eye" frown.

Baurusuchus (bah-er-oo-SOOK-us) was named for the late Cretaceous Bauru formation located in Brazil. Like the living Komodo dragon, *Baurusuchus* ambushed large game from behind rocks and bushes. Rather than having a long, flat skull, this creature had a high, narrow one. It had only a few teeth, but each one was huge and serrated, like those of giant tyrannosaurs. Like all crocodiles, *Baurusuchus* probably shook its victims to death after snagging them on its fangs. Today, only the skull of *Baurusuchus* is known. We can guess the proportions of the rest of its body by looking at the fossils of related land crocs.

TERRISTRISUCHUS (extinct)

Dynamic Dinosaurs

People are fascinated by dinosaurs, but most people can't identify a dinosaur's key characteristics. To be a dinosaur a reptile must have 1) an S-curved neck, 2) a short, straight backbone, 3) knees below its hips, 4) raised ankles, and finally 5) a hole forming the thigh socket in the pelvis. A short, straight backbone and erect legs were adaptations that allowed dinosaurs to continue breathing while sprinting—something that sprawling, wriggling lizards could not do.

Most dinosaurs are so well known that only the recently discovered ones will be unfamiliar to some readers. One of these is the "thorny demon from the River Styx," *Stygimoloch* (sti-jee-MOL-uk). This "bonehead" lived in Montana during the last days of the late Cretaceous period. Other boneheads, or pachycephalosaurs (pak-ee-SEF-uh-loe-sorz), had horns and bumps adorning their "crash-helmet" skulls—but none could match *Stygimoloch* for outrageous attire. Its crown of horns would have served to intimidate rival males or predators. *Stygimoloch* had a tall, narrow dome different from that of other boneheads. Evidently it was used as a battering ram when intimidation failed.

Only the dome and horns of *Stygimoloch* are known. More complete remains from other pachycephalosaurs help us model the probable shape of this beaked plant eater's body.

Hornfaces, such as *Pachyrhinosaurus* (pak-ee-RINE-uh-sore-us), had a different kind of beak, which looked like a parrot's. *Pachyrhinosaurus* grew to eighteen feet in length and is known from a large bone bed in which dozens of these dinosaurs died together during the late Cretaceous period in Alberta, Canada. Pachyrhinosaurs were unusual among horned dinosaurs in not having horns where others did—over the snout and eyes. Instead, thick, raised pads of bone grew over these areas. Useless for goring predators, these thick pads could have been used against rivals, bruising them without killing or wounding one of their own. Horns did sprout from the center of the shield and also from its rim in adult males.

Evidence from the bone bed suggests that this dinosaur grew up fast, taking only five years to mature. *Pachyrhinosaurus* was a forest dweller. Its scissorlike teeth snipped tough, woody food into splinters and chips. Huge jaw muscles originated on the surface of its wide but lightweight shield. As the thinnest part of its body, the frill also served as a heat radiator to help cool the animal after exertion or during the hottest part of the day. The frill and its sideways-pointing horns also shielded the powerful shoulder muscles from attack.

Among the largest and most frightening of all birds was *Phorusrhacos* (foe-rus-RAY-kos), which

lived during the Miocene epoch in the grasslands of Argentina. *Phorusrhacos* was also a dinosaur because, like all birds, it had all of the five characteristics of a dinosaur listed here. Shaped like a tyrannosaur, ten-foot-tall *Phorusrhacos* was the dominant predator of its time. This monster bird had strong running legs and small, useless wings. At the tip of its nineteen-inch-long head was a terrible hooked beak, used for tearing flesh from a carcass.

Phorusrhacids survived until the early Pliocene epoch, seven million years ago, when the previously isolated American continents became linked together at Panama. The cause of their demise remains a mystery.

Many kinds of reptiles, from turtles to duckbill dinosaurs, had beaks instead of teeth. The oviraptorids were beaked dinosaurs not far removed from true birds. *Oviraptor* (oh-vee-RAP-tor), or "egg robber," was the first nonbird dinosaur that had a wishbone (fused collar bones). Its skull was quite unlike that of any other dinosaur. So many holes lightened its skull that mere struts of bone kept it from collapsing. At the top of its head *Oviraptor* wore a hollow crest of bone that was probably a colorful horn-covered decoration, like that of the living cassowary.

Oviraptor also had a strange palate. Instead of being vaulted, it projected down below the jawline and was tipped by two small teeth. This dinosaur was probably a plant eater, sliding its jaws back and forth to slice food held between the beak and the palate. *Oviraptor* lived in Mongolia during the late Cretaceous period, eighty million years ago.

PHORUSRHACOS (extinct)

PACHYRHINOSAURUS (extinct)

STYGIMOLOCH (extinct)

OVIRAPTOR (extinct)

Stupendous Sauropods

More than any other type of dinosaur, sauropods stir the imagination. Sauropods were not, however, the chunky monsters most cartoons and toys portray them to be. They actually looked more like giraffes. Only their bellies were massive, allowing them to slowly digest huge amounts of unchewed plants.

Sauropod limbs supported the body like slender columns. They did not need huge muscles because their leg bones carried most of the weight.

Only their hind feet made the broad, clawed footprints we associate with these dinosaurs. The front feet left small crescent-shaped prints. That is because sauropods had virtually no "fingers." Only the "thumb" bore a claw. Very few tail drag marks are ever found with sauropod footprints. Evidently they almost never let their tails down while walking.

Sauropods had nostrils set high on their heads, rather than at the tip of their snouts as they are often portrayed. The most likely reason for this may be for drinking. Sauropods had to continue breathing while their mouths were underwater.

Recent excavations in China have uncovered a whole new group of sauropods, including *Omeisaurus* (oh-may-ee-SORE-us), named after the sacred mountain, Omeishan. Described in 1984, *Omeisaurus* is known from several incomplete skeletons that have been assembled into one complete individual. This remarkable sauropod grew to sixty-five feet long, including thirty-three feet of neck!

The remarkably long and narrow neck of *Omeisaurus* contained seventeen vertebrae, five more than most North American sauropods. The thin neck, tail, and legs acted as radiators for the heat that built up in this dinosaur's torso.

Like many sauropods, *Omeisaurus* probably stood on its hind legs and tail in order to reach high into the boughs of evergreen trees. *Omeisaurus* lived during the middle and late Jurassic periods, 150 million years ago.

A 1988 report disclosed the rather surprising fact that the tail of *Omeisaurus* ended in a club of bone,

AMARGASAURUS (extinct)

rather than gradually coming to a tip. These sauropods must have swung their tails at their enemies to keep them away.

Like China, Argentina has recently yielded many fine and unusual dinosaurs, including *Amargasaurus* (ah-MAR-gah-sore-us). Named for the Amarga formation, this late Cretaceous sauropod had an unusually high neck and back. Y-shaped vertebral spines elevated the skin along this area possibly creating additional surface area for heat radiation. *Amargasaurus* may also have been more attractive to its mate the larger or more gaudy its neck was. *Amargasaurus* had a long, thin, whiplike tail that would have stung or wounded its adversaries.

OMEISAURUS (extinct)

Terrifying Pterosaurs

Pterosaurs were flying reptiles, closely related to dinosaurs. They were not true dinosaurs because their thigh sockets were cups, not holes. All pterosaurs had wings framed by a greatly enlarged ring finger. The wings themselves were long and narrow, like those of an albatross.

It was once thought that pterosaurs were similar to bats. Recently pterosaurs were thought to have been more birdlike. We now know that pterosaurs walked as birds do on land, but held their legs the way bats do in the air. The wing membranes were very shallow at the elbows and were attached to the body at midthigh. Pterosaurs would have dropped down on all fours only to rest or to cover their eggs.

Northeast Brazil was the home of recently discovered *Tropeognathus* (trope-ee-OG-nath-us), named for its "keeled jaw." *Tropeognathus* was unusual in having a set of crests above and below its snout. Perhaps all pterosaurs relied on their special

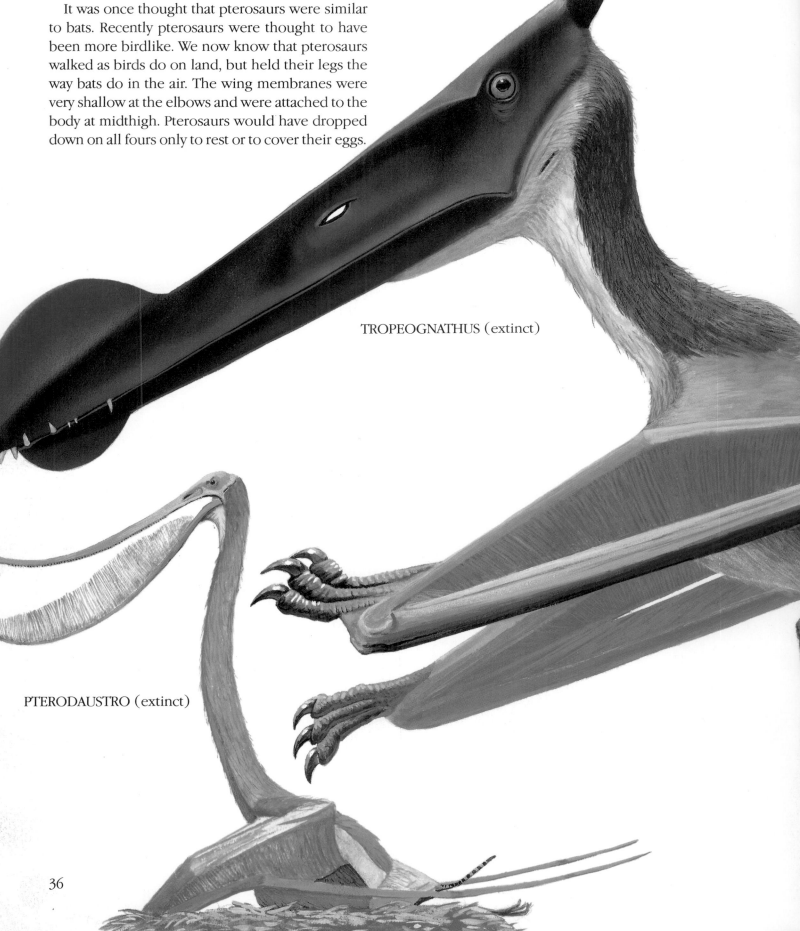

TROPEOGNATHUS (extinct)

PTERODAUSTRO (extinct)

crests to attract their mates. Only the head of *Tropeognathus* is known, but related pterosaurs provide a suitable model for body proportions. It probably had a wingspan of twenty feet. *Tropeognathus* lived during the early Cretaceous period, 112 million years ago, on the shores of the newly formed Atlantic Ocean.

Pterodaustro (tare-uh-DAWS-troe), or "wing of the south," was a much smaller pterosaur that lived during the early Cretaceous period in Argentina. It had incredibly long, densely packed, needlelike teeth on its long, slender lower jaws. This pterosaur probably sifted lake waters for tiny organisms. *Pterodaustro* is remarkable for having, in proportion to its body, the tiniest head and the longest neck of any known pterosaur.

Angustinarhipterus (ahn-goos-tee-nuh-RIP-ter-us), or "narrow fin wing," was a more primitive, Chinese pterosaur. Its huge protruding fangs made a great fish trap. Its long, stiff tail was like that of a dinosaur but was tipped with a small rudder.

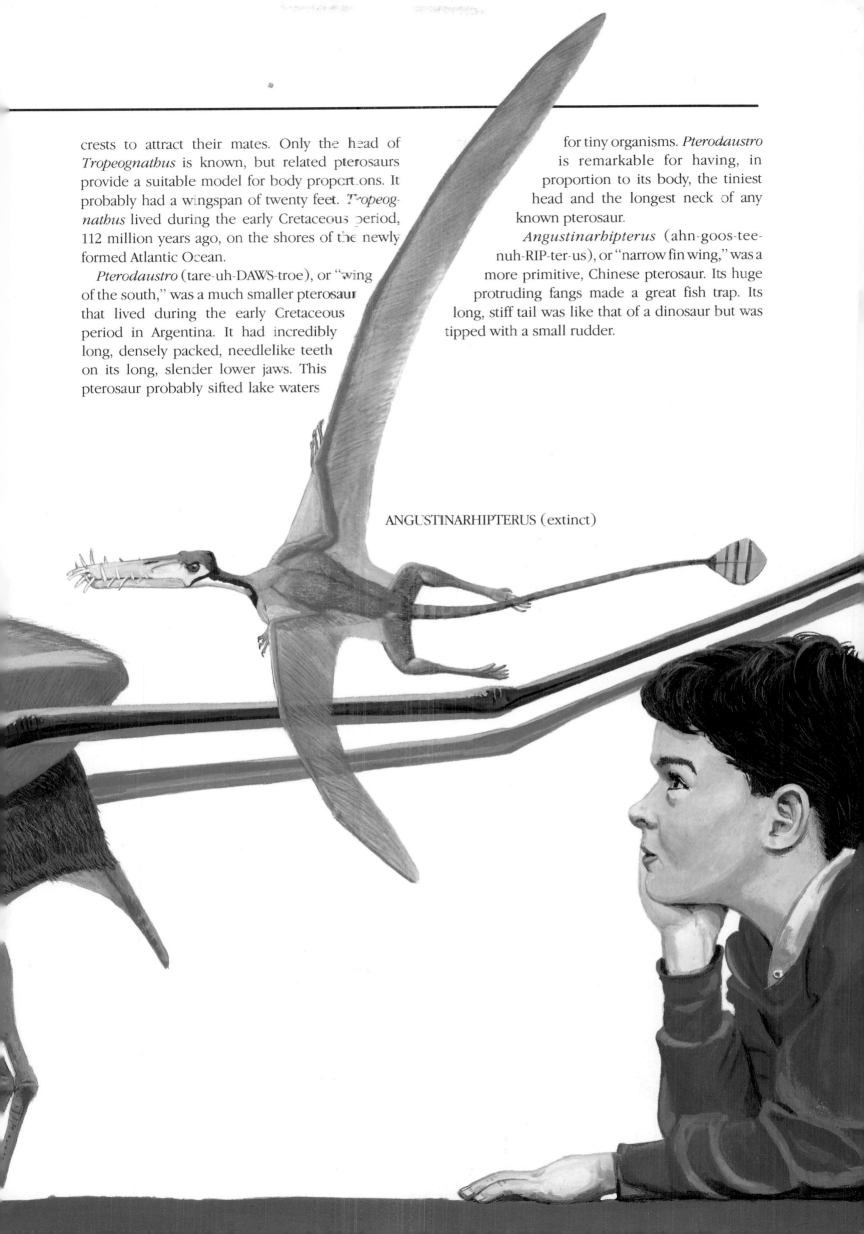

ANGUSTINARHIPTERUS (extinct)

Dangerous Dinocephalians

Everyone knows something about dinosaurs (the "terrible lizards"), but who has ever heard of dinocephalians (the "terrible-headed ones")? Or their parent group, the synapsids?

Both before and after the Age of Dinosaurs, synapsids (sine-AP-sidz) were the dominant animals. The best-known synapsids are the mammals, including humans. The synapsids that lived before the dinosaurs were more reptilian in appearance.

To the rear of the holes that house their eyeballs, synapsids all have one hole in their skull. This hole is filled with large jaw muscles. In humans this hole separates the skull from the cheekbone.

Dinocephalians (die-no-sef-ALE-ee-unz) lived only during the late Permian period. Some of them were among the largest of the early synapsids. They all had rather large, thick-boned skulls, which they used during head-butting contests among rivals for territory or mates. Some dinocephalians were meat eaters; others ate plants. All of them were four-footed and walked with their elbows and knees out to the sides. Nearly all of the dinocephalians that were preserved as fossils lived in Russia or South Africa.

Anteosaurus (AN-tee-uh-sore-us), which means "before the lizard," had a body like that of a very large lizard. But unlike a lizard, *Anteosaurus* kept its belly off the ground at all times, except when sleeping. This lionlike synapsid had a heavy but narrow skull that ended in huge, interlocking bear-trap teeth. *Anteosaurus* had only a few tiny cheek teeth, so this synapsid must have swallowed its prey whole without chewing it first.

Estemmenosuchus (eh-stem-eh-no-SOOK-us), or "crowned with a wreath crocodile," was one of the earliest plant-eating dinocephalians. Like *Anteosaurus*, its front teeth were large and interlocking, but *Estemmenosuchus* was probably more like a prehistoric hippo than like a lion. It may have dredged up soft plants with its protruding teeth. *Estemmenosuchus* had unusual bumps on top of its head and protruding from either cheekbone. *Estemmenosuchus* used its bumpy head to ram rivals and predators. This synapsid was built like a tank, with thick, stout legs and a big belly. Its third eye, the one that pointed toward the sky, was surrounded by a ring of bone for protection against damage.

ESTEMMENOSUCHUS (extinct)

ANTEOSAURUS (extinct)

Dreadful Dicynodonts

Another group of early synapsids that produced a number of large species were the dicynodonts (dye-SYE-no-donts), named for their "two canine teeth." Dicynodonts lived from the late Permian period to the end of the Triassic period, a time spanning fifty million years. Toward the end they lived alongside the earliest dinosaurs and mammals. They were the most numerous, diverse, and long-lived of the early plant-eating synapsids. Their fossils can be found on all the continents, including Antarctica.

Dicynodonts lost most of their teeth and grew a horny beak in their place. Most kept their canine teeth, which grew to resemble tusks. Others were completely toothless. The dicynodont body was short and stout, trailed by a tiny stub of a tail. The forelimbs were massive and splayed out to the sides, but the hind limbs were slender and very nearly erect.

Dicynodonts had quite unusual jaws. They opened and shut, of course, but the lower jaw could also slide forward and back and from side to side to thoroughly mash plants before they were swallowed. Dicynodonts didn't chew their food; they had no chewing teeth. Instead they sheared it to pieces, the way a pair of scissors would, at the tip of the beak and also at the cheeks. Dicynodonts had huge jaw muscles originating from their temples and their broad cheekbones, basically in the same pattern as mammals. They could also continue breathing while moving food within their mouths, something most primitive reptiles could not do.

Dicynodon (dye-SYE-no-don) was one of the first of these synapsids to be discovered, and it lent its name to the entire group. It lived during the late Permian period in South Africa and Tanzania. Dicynodon had a long, low body and rather stubby legs. It probably hid beneath the underbrush, nibbling away at its hiding place.

Placerias (pla-SER-ee-ass) was similar to other large dicynodonts, but it did not have large tusks. Instead a bony portion of its snout became large and sharp, taking the place of tusks. Maybe these, too, offered some protection against predators. Placerias was a common browsing synapsid that lived in the southwestern part of the United States during the late Triassic period. That area was dominated by giant conifer trees and split by small, winding rivers. Now it is a desert and famous as the home of the Petrified Forest.

PLACERIAS (extinct)

DICYNODON (extinct)

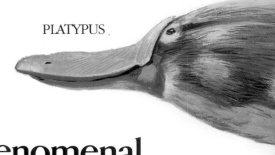

An Irregular Reptile

With its long, toothless beak and its limbs transformed into broad, webbed swimming paddles, *Nanchangosaurus* (nan-CHANG-uh-sore-us) seems to have been the platypus of its day. This enigma of a reptile is known from a single, nearly complete fossil skeleton—yet it has left most scientists scratching their heads. They can't figure out which group this reptile belongs to. The skull of *Nanchangosaurus* is shaped like that of an ichthyosaur (IK-thee-uh-sore) (a shark-shaped swimming reptile), but it has an opening that only archosaurs (crocodiles, dinosaurs, and their kin) are known to have had. Its body most closely resembles that of an unarmored placodont.

Nanchangosaurus had a slender body, heightened considerably by the tall spines of its back vertebrae. Perhaps large swimming muscles originated along these spines, helping this reptile snake its way through the water, probing the muddy bottom for worms and other soft-bodied burrowers. A row of skin-embedded bones topped each vertebra, not for protection but for greater rigidity between the two sets of paddles. Named for the city of Nanchang, *Nanchangosaurus* lived during the early Triassic period in east central China.

The Phenomenal Platypus

The *platypus* (PLAT-ih-pus) is the most unusual of all the mammals. Its name means "broad, flat foot," but that surely is the least of this animal's distinctive characteristics. When it was first brought to the attention of scientists in 1797, the platypus was thought to have been contrived by the joining together of several unrelated animal parts.

Its leathery bill gave it the nickname "duckbill." The bill is used, like a duck's, to sift mud for tiny organisms. The platypus's bill is especially sensitive to underwater movements, which helps it locate prey. Skin folds completely shut off its eyes and ear holes whenever the platypus is submerged. This mammal eats up to 25,000 worms every month, along with crayfish, frogs, eggs, snails, and water insects. Food is packed into cheek pouches before being swallowed along with pebbles that help crush the larger organisms. In place of teeth, the platypus has horny pads.

The platypus propels itself underwater with broad, webbed forefeet. Since the webbing extends

NANCHANGOSAURUS (extinct)

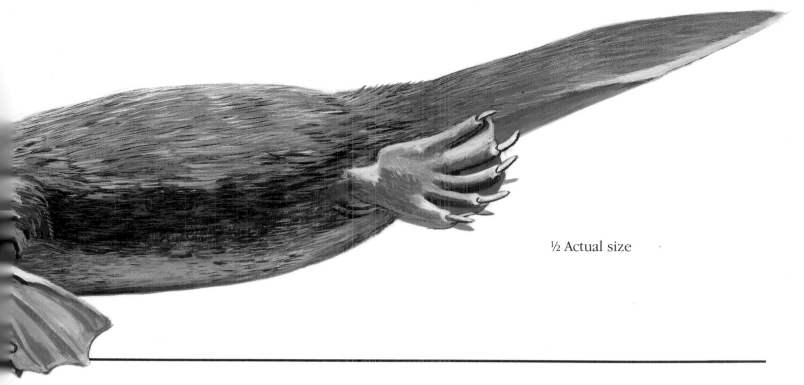

½ Actual size

well beyond its long claws, it folds under the palm, out of the way, whenever the platypus is walking or digging on dry land.

The highly flexible platypus grooms itself by combing its dense fur with the claws of its hind legs. The hind feet of the male platypus are provided with bony spurs—actually modified ankle bones—which can inject poison into enemies (such as rats and river cod) and rivals. No human has ever died from a platypus sting.

The platypus's flat tail acts as a rudder while this creature swims. It is also used like a beaver's tail to tamp down mud around its burrow. In addition, a female may carry a wad of leaves tucked beneath her tail on her way to make a nest.

A platypus builds its nest at the end of a fifty-foot-long tunnel burrowed into the bank of the upland stream in which it feeds. Unlike almost every other mammal, the platypus lays small, sticky, rubbery eggs, usually two at a time. It also urinates and eliminates out of its egg chute, the way reptiles and birds do. (Most mammals have separate openings for these functions.)

The female platypus incubates her eggs by curling around them. When the platykittens hatch,

they are naked and cannot fend for themselves. To feed her hatchlings, the mother lies on her back and milk "sweats" from her milk lines and puddles on her belly. The babies lap up the milk rather than sucking it as most mammals do.

The platypus is the most primitive mammal living today. Its body temperature fluctuates with its surroundings, and its shoulders are more like those of premammal synapsids (see pages 38–39) than those of other mammals.

The platypus can be found today in Tasmania and in eastern Australia in climates that range from tropical to near freezing. Its maximum length is usually twenty inches, but a prehistoric cousin has been estimated to have been at least twice as big.

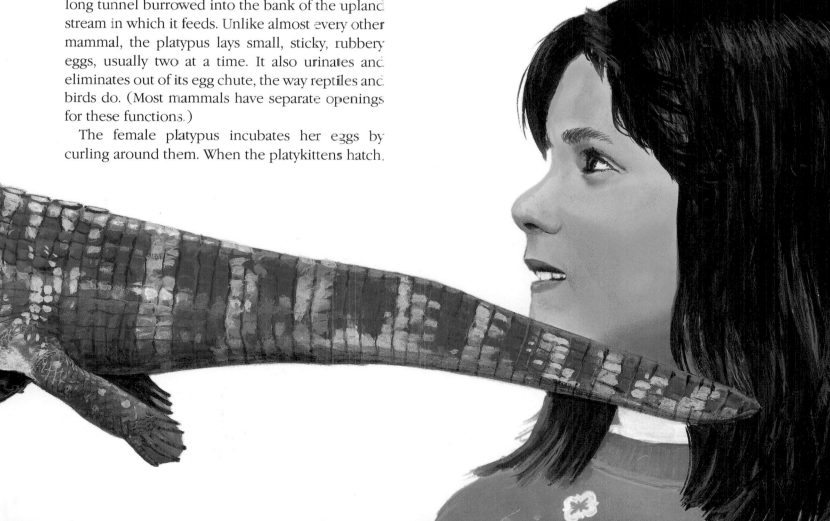

Unusual Uintatheres

Uintatheres (you-IN-ta-theerz), or "Uinta beasts," were among the first large, lumbering, plant-eating mammals. Like later plant eaters, such as cattle and deer, many were ornamented with horns. Uintatheres appeared at the end of the Paleocene epoch, were common during the Eocene epoch, and became extinct thereafter. Their remains are found chiefly in the Uinta mountains of Wyoming and Utah. Another group of uintatheres has been discovered in Mongolia.

Uintatheres are famous for their thick skulls and incredibly minute brains. Fifteen different types of uintatheres are known.

Eobasileus (ee-oh-bas-IL-ee-us), the largest known uintathere, grew to ten feet in length. It was similar in size and build to an African rhino. *Eobasileus* had a pair of long, sharp fangs and three pairs of short, bony horns. The rearmost pair of horns were the largest, sometimes reaching ten inches in length. Uintatheres are sometimes known as the Dinocerata (dye-no-ser-AT-uh) because of these "terrible horns"— used both for inflicting damage on rivals and for impressing females. Males had the largest horns as well as the largest fangs, sometimes up to six inches in length.

Gobiatherium (go-bee-uh-THEER-ee-um), or "Gobi beast," had neither horns nor fangs. This Mongolian uintathere from the Gobi Desert did have huge nostrils and an unusual bony lump over its jutting cheekbones. *Gobiatherium* probably did not charge its adversaries but ran away from danger instead.

A Rare Rhino

Rhinos first appeared in the late Eocene epoch, forty million years ago, in North America and Asia. At first they looked like living tapirs, in both size and shape. All early rhinos were hornless. Then two main types of rhinoceros evolved: a now extinct group of long-legged types and the living group.

Elasmotherium (ee-laz-moe-THEER-ee-um), or "metal plate beast," was nicknamed "the giant unicorn." This rhinoceros had a single horn, which may have been as much as six feet long, growing out of its forehead. The horn itself was not preserved as a fossil because it was made of matted hair, not bone or ivory. The bony base on *Elasmotherium*'s skull tells scientists how large the horn might have been.

Like the living black rhino, *Elasmotherium* had a narrow snout and used its lips to pluck its food. Like the living white rhino, *Elasmotherium* was a grazer. Its molars were very large, to sustain the wear of highly abrasive grass over a long lifetime. *Elasmotherium* lived in the highlands of southern Siberia during the chilly Pleistocene epoch. It probably was hairy, like the woolly rhinoceros pictured in cave paintings.

ELASMOTHERIUM (extinct)

EOBASILEUS (extinct)

GOBIATHERIUM (extinct)

Armored Arsinoithere

Arsinoitherium (ar-sih-no-ih-THEER-ee-um), named for Queen Arsinoë of ancient Egypt, only looked like a rhinoceros. Its horns were actually hollow projections of its skull. They were fused at their base like two huge oak trees growing too closely together. Unlike rhino horns, arsinoithere horns were covered with skin, at least when the animal was young. Traces of blood vessels remain on the surface in fossils. Females had smaller and rounder horns. A second pair of sharp bumps topped each eye.

Arsinoitherium grew to over eleven feet long. It lived during the early Oligocene epoch, thirty-six million years ago, in northern Egypt. What is now a desert was then a lush jungle and the home of some of the earliest apes. This riverside browser had forty-four teeth in its jaws, which is more than the usual number for a plant eater.

Arsinoitheres have no close relatives among living mammals but are distantly related to elephants. Recently some fossil relatives have been discovered, but none of these had horns.

A Unique Unicorn

Related to the musk ox but looking more like a goat, *Tsaidamotherium* (cha-ee-da-moe-THEER-ee-um) was sort of a unicorn. To be sure, it had two horns on top of its head, but they were very unequal in size. The right one was large and centered on the forehead. The left one was tiny and probably useless. Why only one horn? *Tsaidamotherium* probably butted its rivals and enemies with its head, the way modern goats do. A centrally placed horn would have given it as much survival value as two horns placed side by side. An unusual set of horns might also have set it apart from species that could otherwise have been mistaken for it. Many antelopes, goats, and cattle are distinguished by the sort of horns they carry. Among musk ox, goats, and cattle, only the bony horn cores fossilize. The outside horny part of each horn usually doubles the length of the horn core and is not shed, the way antlers are.

Tsaidamotherium lived during the late Pliocene epoch, four million years ago, in Mongolia. It was a grazing animal with high-crowned teeth adapted to chewing tough grass.

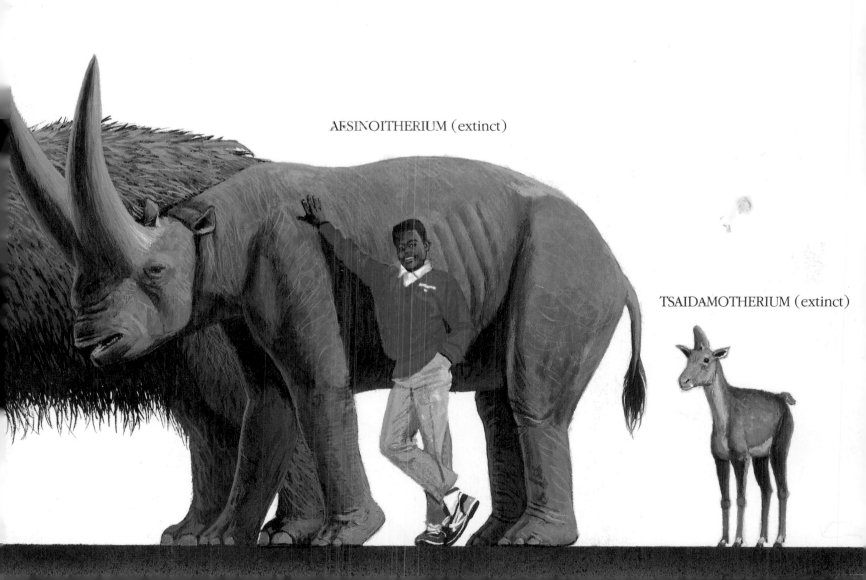

ARSINOITHERIUM (extinct)

TSAIDAMOTHERIUM (extinct)

Exotic Elephants

For their size, their tusks, their trunks, and their ears, elephants are among the strangest of all living mammals. Stranger still were certain prehistoric elephants.

The shovel-tusker *Ambelodon* (am-BEL-uh-don) was an elephant of the late Miocene epoch, twelve million years ago. This ten-foot-tall resident of Colorado and Nebraska roamed the dry grassland prairies much as the modern African elephant roams the savannas. The ancient plains were crossed by many winding rivers that were thick with water plants, *Ambelodon*'s favorite food.

In addition to rather typical upper tusks, *Ambelodon* also had a pair of lower tusks shaped like flat spades. These projected three feet beyond the upper jaw and were used to rip tubers and water plants out by the roots. This elephant, like all others, used its trunk to shove food back to its chewing teeth.

A variety of dwarf elephants lived between the various ice ages, and they are all related to the living Indian elephant. Some have been found on Sardinia, Sicily, Malta, Crete, and Cyprus—all islands of the Mediterranean Sea. Others have been found on the East Indian islands of Java and Celebes. During the ice ages, lowered sea levels provided land bridges to these islands. When the ice melted and waters rose again, certain elephants became isolated on these islands. The smaller elephants survived because they could eat less in a limited area. The smallest dwarf, *Elephas falconeri*, was less than forty inches tall at the shoulder as an adult. Infants were the size of puppies.

The remains of dwarf elephants were probably the source for Greek legends of the Cyclopes, the mythological one-eyed giants that ate people. The dwarf elephant's skull looks like it might belong to a Cyclops because the eye sockets are not prominent and the centrally placed nasal opening looks like it could have been an eye socket.

AMBELODON (extinct)

ELEPHAS FALCONERI
(extinct)

A Grandiose Giraffe

Believe it or not, the long neck of a giraffe is not its most distinguishing characteristic. Giraffes have ossicones, hornlike growths of the skull that are usually covered with skin. All giraffes have unusual teeth, too. They have no upper incisors (nipping teeth), but they do have three pairs of lower incisors, plus canines that are each shaped like an additional pair of incisors. This arrangement gives giraffes a wide set of nippers that work against a bony pad in the upper jaw.

Giraffes are cud-chewing, hoofed mammals, related to deer and antelope. They chew their food, swallow it, and digest it for a while; then the food returns to the mouth to be chewed again and swallowed again. A giraffe spends much of its day chewing cud.

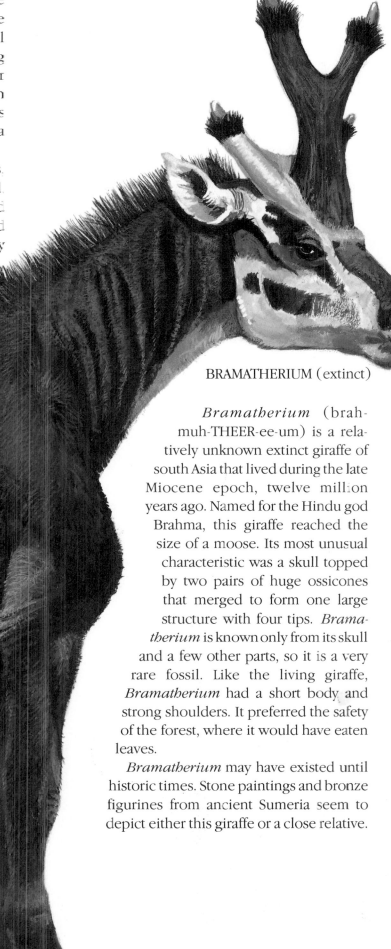

BRAMATHERIUM (extinct)

ELEPHAS
FALCONERI
(infant)

Bramatherium (brah-muh-THEER-ee-um) is a relatively unknown extinct giraffe of south Asia that lived during the late Miocene epoch, twelve million years ago. Named for the Hindu god Brahma, this giraffe reached the size of a moose. Its most unusual characteristic was a skull topped by two pairs of huge ossicones that merged to form one large structure with four tips. *Bramatherium* is known only from its skull and a few other parts, so it is a very rare fossil. Like the living giraffe, *Bramatherium* had a short body and strong shoulders. It preferred the safety of the forest, where it would have eaten leaves.

Bramatherium may have existed until historic times. Stone paintings and bronze figurines from ancient Sumeria seem to depict either this giraffe or a close relative.

Crazy Chalicotheres

Chalicotheres (kah-LEE-koe-theerz) have been described as draft horses with claws. Others were more like a cross between a giant ground sloth and a horse. Chalicotheres were forest browsers, preferring soft leaves to tough blades of grass. Their fossils are rare but have been found on all the northern continents. Chalicotheres became extinct rather recently—only one-and-a-half million years ago.

Chalicotherium (kah-lee-koe-THEER-ee-um) resembled a gorilla because it had very short hind legs, a sloping back, and long, very flexible forelimbs capable of reaching high into the branches for food. *Chalicotherium* seems to have had large calluses on its hips, suggesting that it spent a lot of time sitting. Perhaps it sat beneath trees, reaching up to grasp leaves and bring them to its mouth.

This plant eater was a very slow-moving animal, so its size and claws were its main defense. The bones of *Chalicotherium*'s forearm were fused together, so the arm could not twist the way a human arm can. Its forelimbs did not point straight forward as those of other hooved animals do. Instead they pointed out to the sides. It seems that *Chalicotherium* must have walked on the knuckles of two "fingers," keeping its claws sharp by not letting them scrape the ground. *Chalicotherium* lived during the Miocene epoch, fifteen million years ago, in Europe.

Tylocephalonyx (tye-loe-sef-uh-LON-iks), or "knob-head claw," was a more typical chalicothere. Its body had the proportions of a horse and all four claws pointed forward. They were retractable, like a cat's claws, to keep them sharp. Its skull had an unusual dome of hollow bone, a feature not seen on other chalicotheres. *Tylocephalonyx* could not have reached over its head, as *Chalicotherium* could. It must have reared on its hind limbs to bring its entire body into the boughs of the trees, hooking branches to steady itself. *Tylocephalonyx* lived during the Miocene epoch in North America.

TYLOCEPHALONYX (extinct)

CHALICOTHERIUM (extinct)

Prominent Primates

Primates are mammals specially adapted for life in the trees. Nevertheless, some, including humans, have returned to the ground. Most primates have four long grasping limbs, forward-facing eyes, and a large brain.

The *orangbulunda*, or *proboscis monkey*, is one of the most unusual of all the primates and also one of the rarest. Because its diet consists exclusively of mangrove leaves, this monkey can be found only in the swampy areas of an island off the north coast of Borneo. The proboscis monkey is one of the few primates that can swim underwater. Perhaps the shape of its prominent nose helps keep water out. More importantly, females find the largest noses on males most attractive. A large nose also makes a better resonating chamber when the male honks to announce its territory.

Males may reach sixty-five pounds in weight and rule over a harem of short-nosed females. The enemies of the proboscis monkey include humans, leopards, and crocodiles.

The ferocious-looking *mandrill* is the largest of the baboons and the most colorful of all the primates. The male's massive muzzle has long, fleshy, blue grooves and swellings on either side of a bright red center marking, which expands around the nostrils. Bright blue is caused by clear skin that refracts only blue light. Bright red is caused by blood vessels just below the surface. Females find the colors attractive. Other males find them intimidating.

Interestingly, the same colorful pattern is seen on the male's external genitals, so the mandrill looks the same both coming and going! The female has facial swellings, too, but by comparison they are duller and smaller. When fertile, she has tremendous swellings on her sitting pads.

Like most baboons, the mandrill has enormous canines and long jaws that are used for defense. The mandrill's diet consists mostly of grasses, roots, and tubers. Occasionally one will eat fruit, lizards, hares, or infant gazelles. The mandrill is found today in equatorial west African rain forests.

The fossils of *Gigantopithecus* (jye-gan-toe-PITH-uh-kus) have stirred the imagination ever since they were found in the 1930s in a Hong Kong drugstore. Only jaws and teeth have been discovered so far, but they are far larger than those of any other living primate. Although caution must be exercised in determining body size from jaw size, some estimates put *Gigantopithecus* at nine feet tall.

This prehistoric "King Kong" lived from the late Miocene epoch to at least the middle Pleistocene epoch, one million years ago, in China, Pakistan, and India. It seems to have been related to today's orangutan but was probably a ground dweller. It had small incisors and canines, as humans do. If *Gigantopithecus* walked on two legs as an adaptation to moving easily among the steep slopes of the Himalaya Mountains, then its description would match that of the Chinese wildman, otherwise known as the "abominable snowman." This puzzling beast, known only from eyewitness accounts, dung, scraps of orange fur, and footprints, may be a living *Gigantopithecus*—if it exists at all.

GIGANTOPITHECUS (extinct?)

PROBOSCIS MONKEY

MANDRILL

Index